THE 𝔓SALMS IN MODERN LIFE

THE *Psalms*

IN MODERN LIFE

Sister M. Cecilia, O.S.B.

CHICAGO
1960

HENRY REGNERY COMPANY

Nihil obstat
    JOHN L. McKENZIE, S.J.
        Censor theol. deput.

Imprimatur

✝ ALBERT CARDINAL MEYER, S.T.D., S.S.L.
    Archbishop of Chicago
    May 19, 1960

TO THE GREATEST PSALMIST OF ALL

WHOSE INSPIRED MAGNIFICAT

FIRST HYMNED THE FATHER'S PRAISE

THROUGH HER SON AND HIS

Contents

Third Step: From Life's Natural Level
to New Heights of Cosmic Praise

Psalms: 113	99	96
62	23	148
83	66	149
94	133	150
112	95	

FOREWORD

Despite the ever growing number of translations recently published, the psalms are still largely unknown to Catholics. Even those bound, either by state of life or special pledge, to the recitation of the Divine Office, frequently tend to perform this duty out of routine and not from any conviction that it has a relationship to life's myriad problems. This may be because Christians usually attempt to read Sacred Scripture with minds trained to philosophical abstractions, whereas the ancient writers came to know God by intense personal experience of His help and protection. Consequently, many would-be readers of the psalms soon put them aside protesting they get nothing out of them. Even those who doggedly pursue their reading sometimes get no further than the surface meaning of the words while missing en-

tirely the haunting poetry and the spiritual nourishment to be mined from the deep message these inspired prayers convey.

Furthermore, probably few today realize that the
psalms, precisely because they are God's own Word
to mankind, possess a dynamic element as vital and
timeless for solving the perplexities of modern life
as they were for explaining the problems of those
who first used them. A still smaller minority, so it
seems, grasp the function of the psalms as they are
used by the Church in her Divine Office: to extend
throughout the whole day Christ's own sacrifice of
praise and self-oblation made present again each
morning in the Eucharist. This aspect is of special
importance for those unable to assist at daily Mass,
since they may participate in its effects through reciting at least Prime and Compline from the Divine
Office.

The purpose of this book, then, is to help its readers
surmount the obstacles they may encounter in their
understanding of the psalms. It explains in modern
terms the scriptural background needed to make the
Psalter intelligible. The second part of the book
demonstrates how, through meditating the psalms,
one may open his mind and soul to the very real
spiritual riches of the living Word so as to draw
from it ever greater nourishment. Thus understood
and used, these inspired prayers can lead to an intimacy with the mind and heart of God, an intimacy
that is real, personal, and transforming.

In anticipation of the difficulties caused by strange
oriental images and recondite analogies, the author
has tried to interweave the spiritual experience

which a psalm describes with the inner meaning of that experience so as to prepare the reader for more clearly understanding each group of verses before he comes to it. In this way, one may hope, he will always comprehend what is sometimes unfamiliar reading, interpret the allusions, and so be enabled to see the significance of the whole in regard to his own personal life. All the psalms so treated are quoted in full, obviating the necessity of an additional book.

The text of the Psalter is that sponsored by the Episcopal Committee of the Confraternity of Christian Doctrine. This was selected because it is the one most generally used for the various Offices in English; and also it has the advantage of being arranged in sense lines, which help to bring out the parallelism of Hebrew poetry (cf. Chapter III). All other scriptural quotations, unless otherwise noted, are taken from Msgr. Ronald Knox's translation of the Holy Bible. (New York: Sheed and Ward, 1956).

Grateful acknowledgement is due to many friends who read parts of the manuscript and offered helpful suggestions. Particularly I wish to express my deep appreciation for the assistance of Father Michael Ducey, O.S.B., for his careful criticism of the whole, as also for the invaluable advice of the late Clem Lane, whose great love and use of the Psalms encouraged me to hope that God's Prayer Book was at last coming into its own.

Part One

EXPLORING THE HIDDEN REALITIES
IN THE PSALMS

CHAPTER 1

THE PSALMS ARE A MEANS
TO A FULLER LIFE

ONE OF THE greatest spiritual enrichments the liturgical movement has brought about, together with the present revival of Scripture reading, is a growing realization of the psalms as a precious God-given book showing the best way to commune with God. Many souls, both lay and religious, are taking advantage of this discovery to enlarge their perspectives and deepen their insight into their own spiritual life. This they do either by adopting for daily prayer some form of Office or by using the psalms for meditation. These two modes of usage, far from being mutually exclusive, should rather supplement each other. For when a Christian says the Office, he truly stands before the throne of God as the official spokesman of the Mystical Christ and should for that reason endeavor to make Christ's prayer his own by wholeheartedly embracing the sentiments expressed. This requires that a person become acquainted with the psalms. Although he may find them truly inexhaustible in all their scope and depth, he can, nevertheless, by studying and pondering them, gradually begin to realize something of what they mean, not only to his life of prayer but also to enriching even the very texture of his thinking and everyday living.

The psalms, of course, are difficult to fit into the modern pattern of thought and speech; even a good English translation cannot remove the exotic images and archaic comparisons. But despite all obstacles, these poems are divinely charged with an intrinsic power that functions, as it were, sacrificially, lifting up on the wings of words to the Triune God the worship of heart and lips so as to bring down upon the soul His return gift of life and light. While by their human expression of joys and sorrows the psalms enter into the very substance of ordinary living, at the same time by their divine dynamism they raise even the modern Christian into the realm of supernatural reality, where he may be purified and gradually transformed. For whoever takes upon his lips the very words inspired by the Holy Spirit and used assiduously by the Savior Himself in His earthly sojourn, enters thereby in a very special way into that mystic life on earth of redeeming activity.

The Christian today gains access to that knowledge in depth only through the background of sacred history which prepared mankind for Christ's redemptive work. This is a depth charged with the immanence of the divine element in human affairs; and it is also charged with all the manifestations of omnipotence that are paradoxically mingled with a

tender solicitude—a solicitude which could find expression only in the image of the Good Shepherd.
For instance, in the historical psalms one experiences
God's championing of His helpless people who groan
under the heel of a despotic secularism. Thus one
may realize that souls today also have had an Exodus,
not only when the Lord led them out from under
Satan's dominance through the Red Sea of baptism
but also as He enables each one daily to escape from
the blindness and illusions in which we all live. For
these illusions are what prevent our seeing or ap-
preciating the divine Hand that guides us in our own
exile. If we could but fully realize this fact today,
our lives would embrace a whole new dimension—
the dimension that Christ, the God-Man, revealed
to the world. And we would be able to grasp the
immense possibilities that are ours so long as we
sojourn like pilgrims in a godless world. For the
psalmist tells us:

> When they pass through the arid valley
>   [of this world],
>   they make a spring of it;
>   the early rain [of divine grace] clothes
>   it with generous growth.
>
> (Ps. 83:7)

All this is what the psalms have the intrinsic power
to do—provided one prays them "attentively and
devoutly," whether in the Office or in private com-
muning with God.

In the Office, however, when a Christian stands
as Christ's official ambassador, his petitions and ex-
pressions of adoration have not only the personal

value of what he as an individual puts into them; they also acquire a special weight in consideration of the Person for whom he acts. This means that one can pray the psalms with a two-fold personality: his own and that of Christ, the Son in whom the Father is always well pleased. But he would be no true ambassador who uttered his speeches as if by rote, without ever entering fully into their thought, as so often happens when we say our ordinary prayers. Such a negotiator could not truly plead with effectiveness the interests of his Sovereign. So also a Christian must soon realize how necessary it is that he try to fulfill St. Paul's injunction: "Yours is to be the same mind which Christ Jesus shewed" (Phil. 2:5).

What is the mind of Christ? To judge by His devout Jewish background and also by His many utterances, the substance of the psalms formed the warp and woof of His thinking. How spontaneously they rose to His lips on every occasion, from the temptation in the desert to His dying words on the cross. And during the long nights spent in prayer, how the prophetic verses must have resounded with new overtones on the lips of Him who was even then fulfilling them. So is it not reasonable that, if Christians in their prayer seek the identification implied by using His words upon their lips, they should also endeavor to weave the pattern of His thinking into the texture of their everyday lives?

In these times, however, our thoughts and general reactions are infected inevitably by the miasma of materialism that pervades the very air we breathe. And how often do we halfheartedly seek Christ in prayer with our "faculties bleeding the poison of unsuppressed activity"? Thus we are prone to lose sight of the fact that even the most ordinary things of everyday life are invested by their very nature with the deep spiritual significance indicated by the psalms. Yet this is what gave the added dimension of the Father's will to the least detail of Jesus' own earthly life. Such insight would enable Christians with Him to see the world as "charged with the grandeur of God," to discern His providence guiding their destiny and providing for all necessities, solving their dilemmas by divine intervention, forgiving their transgressions, and testing them by adversities as gold is tried in the furnace. The mind of the psalmist is the mind of Christ, who saw the lilies clothed in God's own shining raiment, the tiny sparrows falling only by His permissive providence, and the Father's loving hand in everything—even to the chalice of His agonizing passion. Thus the psalms will enable men to orient themselves in this world to a more complete reality, if they study these prayers, ponder their meaning, and try to infiltrate into their own minds this ancient but inspired manner of thinking. Then, indeed, their thoughts could become a reflection of Christ's, their words an echo of His, and their acts but a continuation of His redeeming work on earth.

The Psalter and the Mass

In his commentary on the Mass for the vigil of an apostle, Dr. Pius Parsch makes an observation quite pertinent also for the Psalter. Many Introits of the Mass realistically begin with the mind of the individual still absorbed in his own problems and

weighed down by human weaknesses. But as this
soul makes its way through the prayers of the missal,
it becomes increasingly conscious of its union with
Someone far greater and all-encompassing, until at
the Consecration it reaches identification with Christ
in His sacrificial victimhood. In the same way the
Christian today may enter the psalms, if he wants to
use them not only as official worship but also as the
mold of his personal prayer, in order to "put on
Christ." For the Savior in Gethsemane has not only
shown that to advert to one's own troubles and fears
is allowable; He has also given men the very appeals
they may use when overwhelmed by their own cross.
Therefore anyone who is in trouble, in distress, or
plagued by some temptation, or who is crushed to
earth by discouragement, has but to open the inspired Book and say:

> Deign, O God, to rescue me;
> O Lord, make haste to help me.
> (Ps. 69:2)

This means, of course, that the psalms were intended not only for the worship of formal prayer but
also as a God-given channel whereby souls may pour
out their innermost thoughts and feelings, especially
when they seem bottled up by their own inarticulate-
ness with God. Moreover, in many instances, the
psalms give us back the Lord's unmistakeable answer.
In fact, they do even more. Besides grounding the
soul in a spiritual life oriented to Christ and giving it
a divinely ordained means of maintaining that union,
these inspired prayers, if used frequently and with
attention, will enlarge the Christian's horizons and

help him to see life steadily and see it whole, not in two separate compartments of the purely human and the spiritual.

Thomas Merton asserts that merely to recognize one's own personal experience in any given psalm is itself an actual grace. Was it not to this end that the divine Author, who knows and understands all human anxieties and desires, has given a psalm for every mood and occasion of this modern workaday life? For instance, when the daily treadmill takes on the proportions of a Via Dolorosa, one may resort to the consoling thought:

> My help is from the Lord,
>   who made heaven and earth. . . .
> The Lord will guard your coming and your
>   going, both now and forever.
>   (Ps. 120: 2,8)

Likewise when, as happens in the best of circumstances, a soul flinches under the barbed arrows of gossip or of false accusations, it may appeal to Heaven in the very words that Christ Himself must have often used in the losing battle of His public life.

> O Lord, deliver me from lying lip,
>   from treacherous tongue.
>   (Ps. 119:2)

Some may even receive an answer which, like another Angel of the Agony, may not remove the chalice but only strengthen them to drink it. Thereupon these truths will sink into the mind of the sufferer: "What are you, a Christian on earth, but an

extension of Christ? And why does He thus choose
to live on in His members except to carry out His
own redemptive work for the world of today? Therefore is it not fitting that 'the sufferings of Christ . . .
overflow into our lives; but there is overflowing comfort, too' (II Cor. 1:5)? And this comfort lies in
the fact that you are not suffering alone but with
and in Christ—and for a divine purpose." Christians
may even make an ejaculatory prayer of the final
verse of Psalm 119, which Jesus must have used
many a time in His own mortal life. And with what
devastating truth He, the divine Head, could repeat
these very words amid the hatred and scheming of
His contemporaries:

> When I speak of peace,
> they are ready for war.

The Messianic Psalms

Just as in the Mass, the Christian may also enter
into a particular psalm with all the burden of His
own troubles, only to find they are not personal at
all but can be made a part of Christ's redeeming cross.
Therefore, as one reads the psalms, he will find his
own limited perspective gradually enlarged by the
opening of new vistas, new solutions, until he begins
to see himself, as well as the world and all its problems, from the viewpoint of the divine Author. Then
a person's life will have acquired a new dimension,
which will enable him truly to participate with Christ
in the great mysteries contained in the Messianic
psalms. For the soul will then have found that the
vacuum of its self-concern has been filled with a new

sense of oneness—even identification—with the world's Redeemer.

Furthermore, while the members of Christ pray these psalms of the Savior in His passion today, they realize more and more that He has need of their mind and lips and heart to utter and embrace the things that are completing the redemption in His body, the Church. For they with Christ are not only two in one flesh but two in one voice, the voice that cries out from the cross of this modern world in the agony of its redemption now being accomplished. What St. Paul said of himself is true of every consistent Christian today: ". . . in this mortal frame of mine, I help to pay off the debt which the afflictions of Christ still leave to be paid for the sake of his body, the Church" (Col. 1: 24).

This means, of course, that out of the historical details of some psalms may be formed a composite picture which includes present-day circumstances. For instance, the psalmist lamented long ago the destruction of the earthly Jerusalem by the Babylonians:

> O God, the nations have come into your
>   inheritance;
>   they have defiled your holy temple,
>   they have laid Jerusalem in ruins.
>   (Ps. 78:1)

Of this the modern Christian may form a threefold image: (1) the historical destruction of the Holy City on account of the people's infidelity; (2) Jesus on Mount Olivet weeping over the terrible fate of His beloved city because of its rejecting His salva-

tion; (3) Christ in His Mystical Body today uttering
that same lament over the Church in lands where
even now He lies prostrate under the insidious vic-
tories of atheistic communism.

Again, since the Mystic Christ is truly being crucified in His members now on earth, how real becomes
His cry from the cross, while through those who pray
this, He supplicates amid His agony in Communist
Hungary or China, or a Jewish or Negro ghetto
of our "God-fearing" republics:

> My God, my God, why have you forsaken
>   me? . . .
> All who see me scoff at me;
>   they mock me with parted lips, they wag
>   their heads:
> "He relied on the Lord; let him deliver him."
>   (Ps. 21: 2, 8-9)

All this helps to explain how persons who voice
these prayers today can with truth and sincerity take
upon their own lips such an appeal as Psalm 141,
even though they are thankfully aware that they
themselves are not beset by enemies threatening their
life. Rather do they know it is Christ in His members who gives utterance, through this inspired
psalm, to those unspoken appeals rising the world
over. Whether these come from communist torture
chambers or from the fetid slums of our own neg-
lected poor or from the lips of innocent children
segregated by prejudice, it is still Christ who suffers
in His members today. So it is for that same Christ,
now hidden in these mute and helpless souls that
Christians speak when they pray:

> My complaint I pour out before him;
> before him I lay bare my distress.
>
> (Ps. 141:3)

Thus absorbed into the present passion of this Mystic Christ, the soul today soon may find itself swept away on the strong tide of His own utter abandonment of trust, into a kind of peace it has never before experienced. While it weaves the feelings of the suffering Savior, as well as His triumph, into the very texture of its thoughts and words, it too is lifted above the level of passing events and is shown their ultimate meaning in God's eternal Plan. For through the psalms the soul can be purged of its natural self and its earth-bound desires, which it casts into the abyss of redeeming love. To Christ it has been truly joined not only by sharing in the divine life-principle, but also by a united purpose of prayer and self-immolation for the world's salvation.

The Psalms of Praise

Now at last he who has so prayed the Psalter is ready in mind and will to pass through the gates of life-on-the-natural-level into a universe of vastly extended horizons. Here on this completely supernatural plane, where heaven and earth are one, Christians may once more become Christ's heart and mind and voice. This time, however, they join in the unceasing hymn of praise and homage begun in heaven by the Eternal Word but now extended to the farthest reaches of the universe through the Incarnation. For wherever Christ's members on earth realize their highest prerogative, they are saying with the choirs of heaven:

> Praise the Lord from the heavens,
>   praise him in the heights;
> Praise him, all you his angels,
>   praise him, all you his hosts.

(Ps. 148:1-2)

Absorbed as modern men too often must be in workaday affairs, how can they rise to such heights and hymn these praises, not by mechanically mouthing the words but with heart and lips in full accord? Only by clearing the way for God's truth to shine into their souls with all possible intensity. This means that they rouse their minds not only to know Him in all His essence and power but also to recognize how His holiness renders Him worthy of their deepest submission, while His omnipotence makes Him deserving of their unbounded homage. Such worship, though of no intrinsic worth to God, is of paramount importance to man. Msgr. Guardini thus beautifully explains it:

> As long as a person bows his head before his Maker as before one 'worthy' because he is holy and true, that person will be immune to intrinsic deception. ... That is why something must exist in which the truth of the heart can constantly renew itself, in which the spirit can be cleansed, the eye cleared, the character strengthened. And there is: adoration. Nothing is more important for man than to incline his spirit before God,

personally to experience the truth that is
God—this is great and sacred and salutary
for body and soul.[1]

There is yet another way whereby a person may
contemplate God and so praise Him in His glorious
attributes. The psalms remind one over and over
to recognize His infinite beauty reflected in the shining meadow, His wisdom in the movements of the
stars, His joyousness in the sun's giant strides across
the sky, His majesty in the stateliness of the cedars,
His encompassing protectiveness in the solidity of
the hills.

The heavens declare the glory of God,
    and the firmament proclaims his
        handiwork.

(Ps. 18:2)

One is even reminded by the earthquake and the
hurricane to tremble at His righteous wrath.

The voice of the Lord is over the waters,
    the God of glory thunders, . . .
The voice of the Lord strikes fiery flames;
    the voice of the Lord shakes the desert. . . .

(Ps. 28:3, 7)

Contemplating the divine attributes, not in cold
abstract study but in prayer, the soul will find that the
tremendous trifles of its daily life appear as passing
smoke, and all human greatness vanishes like a
dream. Before this absolute power, this matchless

---

[1] Romano Guardini, *The Lord* (Chicago: Henry Regnery Company,
1954), p. 491.

wisdom, this boundless goodness, one is lost in the
abyss of his own intrinsic nothingness. This is an
important reason why the supreme Deity wants His
creatures' praise: not because it is of any benefit to
Him but because it is most necessary for them. It
conditions them to receive His favors. For even the
Omnipotent cannot fill a self-sufficient soul with His
gifts. But if a person, humbled by the reverence that
seizes every created intelligence before the realization of God's infinitude, gives voice in the psalms to
such self-abasement as bowed the very humanity of
Jesus in prayer—then the foundation of the spiritual
life is laid deep and solid. Then God can pour into
such a soul all the graces it needs for "that maturity
which is proportioned to the completed growth of
Christ" (Eph. 4:13).

There is still another reason for the psalms of worship. Man is head of all created things; accordingly,
he has the right and duty to lift them up like a thank
offering in homage to their Maker. This everyone
can do through the psalms. As Thomas Merton beautifully wrote of the wild creatures carrying out their
wordless destiny, "My psalms fulfill your dim un-
conscious song, O brothers in this wood."[1] Thus
modern man may by his intellect and will lift up in
adoration the sun and moon, all the stars, the fire
and hail and storm winds, even the wild beasts and
creeping things, so that all may through his words
and worship pay to their Creator the homage of their
being.

---

[1] Thomas Merton, *Sign of Jonas* (New York: Harcourt, Brace, 1953),
p. 292.

> Praise him, sun and moon;
>> praise him, all you shining stars. . . .
> Praise the Lord from the earth,
>> you sea monsters and all depths;
> Fire and hail, snow and mist,
>> storm winds that fulfill his word. . . .
>> (Ps. 148:3, 7-8)

So it is that the psalms, if sufficiently pondered and assiduously prayed, can immeasurably enrich our modern life. For they are an important factor in integrating all of Christ's thoughts and purposes with the very texture of a person's ordinary outlook. Columba Marmion has called it a fact of experience that with souls who let themselves be replenished by the truths of the psalms the spiritual life is very limpid and sane, and at the same time abundant and fruitful. This is because the secret of all true Christian spirituality lies in the truth that it is derived from the Holy Spirit who uses as His instrument not only the Mass and the sacraments but also the psalms, which He Himself has impregnated with the dynamic power of God's redeeming Word. This means that wherever the psalms are said with reverence and understanding "the Holy Ghost over the bent [soul] broods with warm breast and with ah! bright wings"[2] to bring forth the divine Word, not in flesh but in the human language of our prayer.

---

[2] Gerard Manley Hopkins, *"God's Grandeur."*

CHAPTER 2

THE DIVINE PLAN UNFOLDING

IN THE PSALMS

*A*NYONE WHO HAS really participated in the new Easter Vigil has doubtless discovered that Old Testament events, such as the deliverance of the Israelites from Egypt and their miraculous passing through the Red Sea, contain something of a present reality for the modern world. Thus a person begins to glimpse the peculiarly Christian outlook on history, which sees in all the events of the past, previous to Christ's advent, a series of divine actions, each marking a new stage in the development of that marvelous Design "kept hidden from the beginning of time in the all-creating mind of God" (Eph. 3:9). For whatever was done by the Lord's direct intervention in history was so ordained by Him that those happenings would prepare in a spiritual way for the mysteries to come under the New Covenant of redeeming grace. In such a manner the whole history of mankind before Christ is permeated with the Word of God making ready for Its ultimate expression, when the Word was made flesh and dwelt among us. That coming, together with the Resurrection and Ascension, is the final utterance of all God had to say, the ultimate result of what He intended to do for mankind. Therefore when one reads the Old Testament today, he finds that all the realities of the past—persons, events, even institutions—lead him by their own deepest impulse to the Gospel. This is because they contain in themselves virtualities which, though not at first apparent, gradually unfold the design of infinite Wisdom, a design actualized by the creative continuity of sacred history.

In their use of the psalms for temple worship, the ancient Jews believed that by liturgical re-enactment they could so relive the past as once again to experience its dynamic influence. Likewise, he who prays the same psalms today in an effort to penetrate their deep inner meaning will find, despite their surface materiality and strange modes of expression, that the great deeds of the past have a definite impact upon his own spiritual life. For the psalms, being the work of the living Word, are directed toward the actual life of every epoch, in order to establish with each human soul the personal relationship that the God of love has desired from the beginning. Just as the brazen serpent, the type of the redeeming Christ, was not a lifeless statue but one imbued with supernatural power, so also the actual words of the psalms are manifestations of the Word. Such revelations—when given by inspiration to men of flesh—are ever active and dynamic, pulsing with the vigorous energy of the Word's own divine life. Never static, they are permeated with a living tradition based on the needs and problems of each era. Therefore, to know the psalms as dynamically alive in this modern age, to come into contact with their vitalizing power, one must learn to see—deep within the ancient events or problems that they relate—the corresponding events and problems of today lying, as it were, in embryo. It must be remembered that the psalmist of old received God's message in a living word that was as closely in touch with the then practical concerns of men as the Lord Himself was when He personally guided His people during their long wanderings in the desert. This is why the psalms have always been understood to have deep significance for the here and now of every epoch and nation. This is why the Christian today, like the Jew of old, does not pray about the great deeds of a past dead and gone. Rather he is thinking of those events as living realities with an immediate impact on his own life. Thus, for instance, he is made fully aware of all that is implied for him by the deliverance of the Jews from Egypt as a redemptive act whose "sacramental signs" are made manifest for him, not only by the rite of baptism but also by his own complete severance from the old life and his entering into a new and supernatural mode of existence.

Daniélou has observed that "before granting the plenitude of revelation to his people, he [God] began by familiarizing them gradually with his ways."[1]

---

[1] Jean Daniélou, S.J., *The Lord of History* (Chicago: Henry Regnery Company, 1958), p. 5.

Such a divine education would benefit even Catholics today, who could thereby acquire a deeper appreciation of the Eucharistic Presence by learning how long and how carefully God had prepared His people for the incredible condescension of personal companionship with Him who dwells "in unapproachable light" (I Tim. 6:16). This He did—first through the pillar of cloud and of fire, then by the throne above the Ark, and the temple "wreathed in cloud" (III Kings 8:10)—until at last the "hour" when the Word Himself "was made flesh and pitched his tent among" men. Thus Christians of today, making their own prayer those Hebrew psalms of longing for the ancient temple, may attain a deeper sense of gratitude for the Real Presence in their churches, which are more truly than any temple of old "the dwelling place [of the] Lord of Hosts" (Ps. 83:2). Only such an insatiable craving for the Eucharistic Presence— permanent and wholly spiritual, yet itself but a preparation for that of the City whose temple is the Lamb —can nourish the desire of modern man in his thirst for God and for its present fulfilment.

This is one of the many reasons why the prayer of Israel so naturally became the Church's prayer, since the aim of the Old Testament was to prepare souls of desire. And the psalms are the prayer inspired by the Holy Spirit in order to teach men of all times how to yearn and so to ask for those things God most wants to give. So it has ever been that each new generation, while praying the psalms, has felt itself caught up in the life of those living words, while the divine Word itself, answering men's need to commune with their Maker, has responded as a vital power to the exigencies and problems which beset each epoch in world history.

In the psalms, which have well been called a compendium of the whole Bible, revelation is not developed systematically, as in science or mathematics, by the progressive building up of new truths. On the contrary, God's revelation through Scripture resembles a musical theme, first expressed simply, as in the Exodus story, then repeated again and again, enriching itself all the while by contrapuntal effects and new harmonies, until it becomes a world symphony, filling the whole spiritual universe. So it is that through the deepening of the truths revealed from the very beginning, the psalms bring together and exalt by means also of imagery and poetic evocation, the clearly marked lines of the Great Design. For example, they tell in terms of an earthly realm about the splendor of that everlasting kingdom already established, not by the exploits of a king subject to human frailties, but by David's Son begotten by an eternal Father "before the daystar" (Ps. 109:3).

By the victory of His redeeming sacrifice the New Moses even now leads His people to their conquest of the Promised Land through a world beset with relentless foes and enticements. Even after their apostasy to worship the vain idols of passing time, He brings them back to repentance, restoring them from exile and giving them a new heart by the power of His sacraments. In this our day, when the agelong struggle seems to be reaching another climax in the death throes of a worn-out epoch giving birth to a new era, that same Redeemer stands revealed in the psalms as the invincible champion of His people,

directing their way through the desert of secularism
and pessimism, sustaining their life, and crushing
their foes. Indeed, the historical psalms have much
to teach men today about the meaning hidden in our
trials and sufferings; and they also give us the surety
of a Wisdom and Goodness that have never failed His
own whenever they came to Him in utter trust and
in true sorrow for sin.

Not only do the psalms tell of past events and their
significance for the present; they also reveal the future
even to the consummation of the divine Plan. The
prophet Isaias (51:9-10) discerned his people's mysterious supernatural destiny far above and beyond
what man alone could ever descry. Isaias' vision
reached from the Red Sea episode through the "As-
syrian flood." Where Isaias left·off, the modern Christian, by aid of the *Apocalypse,* can follow the prophetic unfolding even to the borders of eternity.
Just as the ancient seer could perceive the ransomed
exiles returning home from Babylon with joyous
psalms on their lips, the Christian, supporting himself on revealed reality, can make the projection of
that past into the future, and so reach out to unknown
things yet to come. Thus he will find that God's
miraculous interventions in history are also the pledge
of another and final liberation of His people at the
end of time. For "each redemptive act of God not
only had dynamic power in the present moment; it
was also a pledge of *the* great redemption of the future."[1] Therefore man today, when standing at the

---

[1] Carroll Stuhlmueller, C.P., "The Influence of Oral Tradition Upon
Exegesis," *The Catholic Biblical Quarterly,* XX, No. 3, p. 311.

junction of the Old Testament and the New, can see
the seeds of those great historic deeds flowering into
New Testament prophecy about that final Act that
is to complete forever the Great Design "hidden from
all the ages and generations of the past; now, he has
revealed it to his saints" (Col. 1:26). For the psalms
contain simultaneously with the past and present
the reality of that final consummation, the New
Jerusalem, which is to be the everlasting "tabernacle
pitched among men; he [God] will dwell with them;
and they will be his own people, and he will be
among them, their own God" (Apoc. 21:3).

In the ancient temple services the people felt that
by the liturgical recital of God's saving acts they were
themselves being drawn into a sharing of that divine
activity. Therefore, they regarded God's inspired
word in the psalms, not as a dead letter but as a living
source of power. It is not surprising, then, that the
Church, the very Body of the living Word-made-
Flesh, also ceaselessly hymns that Word, once given
by inspiration but now living on within her as spirit
and life. So it is that each repetition of these prayers
could mean for the thoughtful reader today progressive discovery of new meanings, a transposing of the
transitory into its eternal significance. Only in the
light of the New Testament can the hidden content,
the ultimate import of each Old Testament event, be
made known. Yet, on the other hand, the psalms,
showing as they do God's way of preparing and teaching mankind, add to the mysteries of the new dispensation a greater depth.

For example, the nature psalms may remind the
Christian of the significance of this fact, that the

omnipotent Creator did not form man in Paradise. But through fatherly love God placed him there later to rest in a garden, which was the sanctuary of the divine presence. Many psalms take up the theme that, after the Fall, the Lord formed another Adam— the Chosen People—whom He brought into the Promised Land, which was also a garden full of all earthly delights. Unlike the first man, however, David and his countrymen could not attain their rest without fighting for it. But it is more than a coincidence that the great warrior-king enters Sacred Scripture, not with a sword but with a harp; he achieves his spiritual conquest, not by blood but with psalms on his lips. And so with the war cry *Israel* ["God fights the battle"], he makes every event in his life—all his struggles, sorrows, joys, and triumphs —a sacred song, not for his own glorification but that God's kingdom may be established in the hearts of his people.

All this background adds a wealth of meaning to the fact that Christ, too, when He returned victorious over sin and death, placed men of the new creation in a garden, His Church. Yet the Christian today well knows that he too, like David, must conquer enemies from within and without before he can enter his rest, which is the peace of Christ. The modern man should also discover that, since the battles of the soul are won by spiritual weapons, he likewise would fight best with psalms on his lips, knowing that such is the Christan strategy. So the great Apostle of the Gentiles saw it: "May all the wealth of Christ's inspiration have its shrine among you; . . . now there will be psalms, and hymns, and spiritual music, as you sing with gratitude in your hearts to God" (Col. 3:16).

There are several basic ideas sown in the Old Testament like seeds—virtualities that gradually bloom into enduring reality. Of these the most important is the concept of the People of God, whose intrinsic unity was first suggested as far back as the call of Abraham with his promise of a posterity sprung from a single source. Then the idea became a physical reality in the desert, where the covenant was made and ratified between the Almighty and the Jews acting as a single entity. But this heterogeneous mass of individuals—both good and wicked, weak and strong—often broke its solemn covenant and fell into the worst abominations of idolatry. Consequently, the Lord at length destroyed Jerusalem, permitting the survivors to be led into captivity. There in exile the "remnant" became through suffering a "new people" created afresh by having been given "a new heart . . . [with] a new spirit" breathed into it (Ez. 36:25). Thereupon it was permitted to return home and rebuild the temple, created and consecreated anew by the divine Presence.

All this might be mere history, were it not given depth and significance by the New Testament, which continues the same theme even to Calvary, where that "remnant," now reduced to One Faithful Servant, is finally rejected by Israel. But risen to a new and deathless life, that same "remnant" becomes the vital trunk on which St. Paul perceived a new progeny grafted into divine life to the forming of a universal People, the Church. Last of all, St. John, pursuing the theme still further, glimpsed a final view of the People of God surrounding the throne of the Lamb. "And now it was a new hymn they sang: . . . Out of every tribe, every language, every people, every nation thou hast ransomed us with thy blood and given us to God" (Apoc. 5:9).

Likewise, the germinal idea of the Kingdom of God in Sacred Scripture undergoes an evolution that incalculably enriches its meaning. Conceived in the Jewish mind as the dominance of Israel, by divine protection, over all its rivals, the concept gradually deteriorated even more into a notion of the immunity of God's people while His justice was being poured out on the surrounding nations. Such a misconception was corrected by the prophets, who warned the Jews that extraordinary favors brought a corresponding weighty obligation on their part; or else the Jews themselves would be the first on whom the divine justice would fall. Yet those ancient seers, after the old and sinful life would have been obliterated in the overwhelming catastrophe that destroyed the temple, often mingled with the thought of divine wrath the far-off vision of a transfigured world to be realized at least in type. Accordingly, after the "seventy years of captivity," a humble and chastened "remnant" came back from Babylon to re-establish a new and better kingdom, a truer figure of that which Christ was one day to establish.

The song of the returning exiles, Psalm 125, is truly a prelude to the joy that should reign in the world today. For our modern world holds even now the real kingdom established by the Savior's death and resurrection. This means that "the coming of Christ has brought the kingdom of God into being. The only real society now is that of God's people, the Church. Christ's universal and exclusive kingship is an accomplished fact."[1] Yet it is likewise true that earthly societies and civilizations do continue to exist, driven by the thirst for power and the passion for gold. That is because this is the period of grace given to men that they may choose for all eternity whether they will give their allegiance to Satan's dominion or to Christ's. Only after all have been so tested, will that cry resound from the battlements of heaven: "The Lord our God, the Almighty, has claimed his kingdom; let us rejoice and triumph and give him the praise" (Apoc. 19:6-7).

St. Augustine asserts that the deep reverence paid by Israel to the kingship was not so much to what the office was in itself but rather to the fact that it "foreshadowed one that should last forever. . . . The very oil with which he [the king] was anointed . . . must be understood symbolically as pointing to a profound mystery."[2] This fact is all the more striking in that the king of Israel was not a legislator, since the Law had already been divinely given. Nor was he primarily a military leader; the very name *Israel* means "God fights the battle," as was well proved throughout the wars of conquest preceding the monarchy. Since the first king was enthroned only after peace had been established, his function was above all to realize, so far as possible, the reality of

---

[1] Jean Daniélou, S.J., *The Lord of History* (Chicago: Henry Regnery Company, 1958), p. 16.

[2] St. Augustine: *The City of God,* Book 17, chap. 6.

God's reign on earth. This is why in the psalms David —although a typical oriental potentate—is transformed by the inspiration of the Holy Spirit into a King of Glory. For in him the sacred poets saw the Lord of lords, the Almighty Ruler, to whom belongs all homage and adoration in heaven and on earth. Such a conception of the kingship has always been the pattern for our own idea of Christ. This is readily seen in our worship of Christ the King: the King of kings, arrayed in all celestial splendor after His victory over the Prince of this world—His throne, the cross.

Therefore, all Christians have perceived in David —too human though he was in the weak flesh—a figure of Christ, both in royal splendor and in suffering. For instance, in Psalm 3 the king, hunted by his son Absalom, is merged into the reality of Jesus hounded by His enemies. Even more, the picture enlarges into the whole Mystic Christ today persecuted in His members. Thus the psalm easily becomes, on Christian lips, Christ's own appeal for divine aid on behalf of His suffering members the world over. Even David's sins belong to Christ in the sense that Isaias meant when he wrote: "God laid on his shoulders our guilt, the guilt of us all" (53:6). Thus the sinning king's psalms of penitence become the voice of the sinless Savior endeavoring to cleanse and purify His Mystical Body on earth today.

Especially significant is the episode when David, wanting to build a dwelling place for God received this answer through the prophet Nathan: "Not David will build the Lord a house, but God will build David a house. It will be a gift of God's grace. It will not be a house of stone, however. It will be another 'man according to God's heart,' the 'Son of David.' "[1] We today know that the Lord was to build a temple such as David had never even conceived. For it was only in the light of the New Testament that the Son of God, who was of David's flesh, proclaimed Himself a temple, which when destroyed He would raise up again in three days. Moreover, the temple of the risen Christ is not built by hands but constructed of living stones. "Apostles and prophets are the foundation on which you were built, and the chief corner-stone of it is Jesus Christ himself. In him the whole fabric is bound together, as it grows into a temple, dedicated to the Lord; in him you too are being built in with the rest, so that God may find in you a dwelling-place for his Spirit" (Eph. 2:20-22). Therefore, the ancient temple worship, for which most of the psalms were composed, will only find its full meaning and consummation in the heavenly liturgy of the Whole Christ before the throne of His Father.

The inspired psalms have made it possible, then, for man of the modern world to actually participate in the sacred history they reveal. For every event in his life today—its struggles, disappointments, triumphs, even failures—may become through these prayers part of the progressive workings of the Word seeking man in order to form him into the People of God. And if the psalms ever impress anyone as out of keeping with the average life because they sing

---

[1] Damasus Winzen, O.S.B., *Pathways in Holy Scripture: The Second Book of Kings* (Elmira, N.Y.: Mount Savior Monastery, p. 3.

so much of warfare and strife, be it remembered that they are as applicable to man's conflict with the powers of darkness as they were to internecine war. And how encouraging are those battle hymns in the lifelong struggle! For they always portray God as the Great Protagonist, whose victory, won once for all objectively, awaits only the individual soul's full cooperation in order to bring that soul's conflict to a successful conclusion. Again, in praying the psalms we participate in the many trials due to the sins of man, until we learn that now as always on God's part, all is forgiving grace. This is the theme expressed in most of the psalms, from the simple statement, "In my distress I called to the Lord, and he answered me" (Ps. 119:1), to the great theophany of Psalm 17:

> From the brightness of his presence
>   coals were kindled to flame. . . .
> He sent forth his arrows to put them [my
>   foes] to flight,
>   with frequent lightnings he routed
>   them. . . .
> He reached out from on high and grasped
>   me;
>   he drew me out of the deep waters.
> He rescued me from my mighty enemy
>   and from my foes, who were too powerful
>   for me.
>   (vv. 13, 15, 17-18)

It should be evident, then, from all the foregoing, that the Christian in the world today who would grasp subjectively all the meaning contained in the psalms

must use them intelligently and assiduously in order
to nourish his life of personal prayer. In this way he
may gradually come to recognize and receive ever
more fully the Word with all its vitalizing effects on
his soul. For the truths expressed in the psalms have
but one aim: to establish the personal relationship
which God desires to have with every human creature. This is the work of the living Word to be found
therein. Consequently it is true that those who pray
these inspired hymns have the Word actually upon
their lips, and likewise within their hearts. Theirs
is the privilege of experiencing in all actuality that
glorious Presence, ever luminous and vitalizing,
which was manifested to Israel in the form of a
pillar of cloud. Once it filled the ancient temple with
glory, and it dwells in souls today as truly as once it
abode above the Ark—the "sacrament" of its unceasing companionship.

Nowhere more than in the Psalter is there such
potentiality for attaining that intimacy with the Lord
for which humanity yearns. Here the one who prays
is raised by divine power to the supernatural level
of an interchange between the Word once spoken to
man and now returned on the wings of faith to its
Source in the Godhead. Such a *commercium*, however, requires a living faith that sees all reality—past,
present, and to come—permeated with the power of
God carrying out His loving Design "to give history its fulfilment by resuming everything in him
[Christ]" (Eph. 1:10). And in that fulfilment the
psalms will reveal "how rich God is in mercy, with
what excess of love he loved us: . . . and he, in giving
life to Christ, gave life to us too; . . . raised us up

too, enthroned us too above the heavens, in Christ Jesus" (Eph. 2:4-6). He who prays thus, his mind enriched by all the significance of the past, and his horizons expanded by faith into eternity, will find his present life immeasurably more full of meaning. For he now feels himself being "filled with all the completion God has to give," here in life's desert proving ground (Eph. 3:19).

CHAPTER 3

HEBREW POETRY AS AN AID
TO PRAYER

*A*LTHOUGH HEBREW poetry, as found in the psalms, differs greatly from that to which the modern reader is accustomed, it still has one feature in common with all great art: it is the expression of a soul attempting to share with others a living experience so tremendous as to exceed the boundaries of prose. Such poetry is necessarily permeated with the consciousness of a vital, personal relationship with the living God, a relationship that cannot but lift the mind and soul on the wings of prayer. Emotional though it may be, there is something more than sentiment here; rather a heart-outpouring that is dynamic and impregnated with life. For the poet is but the instrument through which acts a Power transcending all human thought and experience—the Holy Spirit Himself. This is the ingredient of the psalms that gives amazing reality to the singer's sense of God's nearness to man, that makes every obstacle to such reality vanish like snow under the burning sun of man's faith.

Most of the psalms are lyric in the sense that they express the whole scale of emotions so universally human that even today a person may read their outpouring and say within himself: "I too am alive in this, personally expressed in it." That is because the Psalter contains truly all the music in the heart of mankind when swept like a harp by the hand of its Maker. For only the Spirit of God knows that heart so intimately as to draw forth from it such lyric bursts of tenderness, solemn strains of penitence, plaintive melodies of grief, or even such exultant paeans of victory. These themes and many more through the psalms are for all men a living actuality, in that they have truly expressed the life experience of all generations and cultures for three milleniums.

Yet the psalms do far more than merely express a complete range of human feelings; they are a divine catharsis for the heart overcharged with passion. For example, in the so-called cursing psalms, like 108, the soul may give utterance to all its pent-up resentment, while at the same time coming to realize that not itself but Christ is the actual target of the wrongs it suffers, since such is the oneness within the Mystical Body. In this way, self-centered indignation can become righteous wrath for God's honor. This is why the ancient Hebrews used those imprecatory psalms as national anthems expressing not an individual's but a nation's anger. For their great love of God, commensurate with their love of country, was the flame that lighted their hatred for Israel's foes. Also the *Miserere*, Psalm 50, which was David's prayer of contrition for his sins of murder and adultery, on Christian lips is not only a sincere expression of sorrow for sin, but it may also act as a healing remedy and aid to salvation.

The psalmist's outlook on life is especially good for persons of this present day, when secularism has so tinged even Christian thought as to obscure the vision which sees life as an integral whole. The ancient poet, on the contrary, beheld everything—his past history, his natural surroundings and human activities —as under the guiding hand of an all-wise and omnipotent Deity. Thus in the psalmist's meditations he saw his people's past transfigured by the momentous interventions shaping history according to a divine plan. Then, too, pondering the lofty insights of prophecy, he was able to bring these insights down to the terms of common everyday life, where they could be felt and applied. In such a fashion the psalms became the folk songs of Israel, as it integrated everything in its daily life with God. So the people made sacred their harvest festivals with hymns that lifted men's minds from material things to their bountiful Giver. Wedding processions, too, were rendered reverent as well as joyous in being God-centered; while their work songs became robust and virile with the religious aspirations of the laborers.

The temple services, above all, stirred the poet's soul to every possible expression of devotional outpouring. As David himself in an ecstasy of joy danced before the Ark of the Lord's Presence, so on the great festivals of the year the psalmist summoned all musical instruments as a reinforcement for Israel's choirs to "sing joyfully to God our strength" (Ps. 80:2). Although the ancient poet did not yet even know of the eternity of bliss awaiting him, his songs of homesickness for God's earthly temple, with its merely symbolic sacrifice, should arouse in Christian hearts a greater realization of the surpassing privilege they enjoy. For theirs is easy access to the one supreme Sacrifice of redemption, in which heaven and earth are joined in the highest liturgy of homage and adoration. But if long familiarity may have quenched modern man's appreciation of all this, then the psalmist's yearning may again light the fire of longing in the flame of such sublime poetry as this:

> O God, my whole soul longs for thee,
>   as a deer for running water;
> My whole soul thirsts for God, the living
>   God; ...
>
> Memories come back to me yet, melting the
>   heart;
>   how once I would join with the throng,
>   leading the way to God's house,
>   amid cries of joy and thanksgiving.
>   (Ps. 41:1, 5, Knox Version)

That such spiritual and emotional exaltation demands for its vehicle some poetic form goes without saying. In the psalms, however, such form is not at first apparent. Yet, although completely lacking in rhyme and meter according to modern standards, they do give the impression of some rhythm when recited aloud in choir, an effect due to the more or less regular pause at the asterisk, which functions as a caesura. The verse structure also contains another feature, the real constitutive element of Hebrew poetry, which the sense-line translation used in this book plainly reveals. That outstanding feature is parallelism, which seems to have been divinely planned as an aid for meditation.

Hebrew poetry expresses a thought, not in one sentence but in two or more parallel clauses. This means that most verses consist of balanced couplets, wherein usually the second half echoes the first couplet or expresses an exactly opposite thought. Here is an example of the first or *synonymous parallelism,* which abounds throughout the psalter:

> Gird your sword upon your thigh, O mighty
> one!
> In your splendor and your majesty ride on
> triumphant.
>
> (Ps. 44:4)

The second or *antithetical parallelism* is illustrated by this verse:

> For the Lord watches over the way of the
> just,
> but the way of the wicked vanishes.
>
> (Ps. 1:6)

Sometimes, too, the poet uses a *progressive parallelism* in which the second part of the verse explains or develops the thought expressed in the first. For instance:

> The Lord is near to all who call upon him;
> to all who call upon him in truth.
>
> (Ps. 144:18)

Then also the reader may be drawn upwards by a *climactic parallelism,* which in a stairlike movement brings the mind to truths not at first visualized. Psalm 120: 1-4 is an excellent example of such a mental ascent from the soul's merely looking toward the mountains as symbols of God's help to its comforting repose in the knowledge that He who keeps Israel "neither slumbers nor sleeps." Also in the prelude to Psalm 28 there is an illustration of this climactic effect. The triple repetition of *an offering to the Lord* lends the invitation ever more urgency, while the second half of each line adds a further step toward the summit of that "worship in spirit and in truth" foretold by the Savior Himself (John 4:23).

> Sons of God, make your offering to the Lord;
>   an offering to the Lord of honour and
>   glory,
>   an offering to the Lord of the glory that
>   befits his name;
> Worship the Lord, in holy vesture habited.[1]

In many ways, then, the psalmist, through the parallelism of his poetry, examines an experience or idea, as one would a precious stone, turning it this way and that in order to reveal its radiance in every gleaming facet. So too he often holds up to the light of the mind some valuable teaching under various images, illumining it from many different viewpoints, until he has explored the full extent of its meaning. This

---

[1] Taken from the Knox Version. Since the psalms are here being considered as poetry, the author has selected those translations that best illustrate this quality.

38 *The Psalms in Modern Life*

is why the psalms are eminently suited to our modern age. Such pondering tends to slow down the frenzied tempo of minds geared to an efficiency based on speed, while the close examination of a thought in its varied aspects will give a person pause to dwell a little longer on some great truth, for the purpose of assimilating it more thoroughly. This in itself is a form of meditation, an exercise the psalms urge again and again as necessary for any spiritual progress.

> Happy the man who . . .
>   delights in the law of the Lord
>   and meditates on his law day and night.
> (Ps. 1:1-2)

Another poetic device that could be used as an aid to meditative prayer is the *refrain*. Anyone familiar with group singing knows the value of recurring words with their added attraction of a growing familiarity. Bishop Sheen once adverted to the psychology of this fascination for the familiar under the title, "The Thrill of Monotony." Likewise, the ancient psalmist understood the value of the human appeal of the refrain, which often lingers in memory long after the rest of the song has faded away, thus making an excellent formula for frequent aspirations during the day. In the psalms the device has an additional use and significance. At the end of each succeeding strophe, or stanza, the refrain should express a deepening of mood and insight, which have been enriched by the thought and feeling that preceded it. This principle is abundantly illustrated in Psalms 41-2.

Others using a refrain are 45, 56, 61, 66, 79, and 135; the refrain to Psalm 135 is in the form of a litany.

Symbolism and Imagery in the Psalms

Another quality of great poetry is its power to find access through the visible world to a higher—even a transcendent—plane. The Hebrew psalms possess this faculty to an eminent degree, being essentially a revelation of the divine through the things of visible creation. Such symbolism or analogy should be especially helpful to persons reciting the Office in Latin or even in English, if in choir. Whereas an abstract truth would be largely lost in the rapid recitation, the mind can use a concrete image associated with that idea to recall the depth of meaning in the thought so conveyed. For example, Psalm 147 paints an exquisite picture of the alternating seasons and their resulting aspects in nature, first under winter's pall of snow and then when the Almighty, breathing upon the frozen streams, sets them free again to revivify the earth. This striking image should always remind the reader that God's moral law, just as immutable as nature's, is not subject to any evolutionary process. But what a lovely image conveys this truth!

Now he spreads a pall of snow,
    covers earth with an ashy veil of rime,
Doles out the scattered crusts of ice,
    binds the waters at the onset of the frost,
Then, at his word, all melts away;
    a breath from him and the waters flow!

This is the God who makes his word known
      to Jacob,
   gives Israel ruling and decree.
                              (Ps. 147:5-8)[1]

Or again, the truth of divine omnipotence is so
overwhelming that it staggers the mind and leaves
but a vague idea. In Psalm 41, for example, a person
sees that same power of God imaged in the Jordan's
thundering cataracts, he actually experiences God's
infinite potency and the realization of man's finitude.
Furthermore, there may be found in Psalm 94 two
key words that contain a vivid image of great significance for the Christian today: *Meriba* and *Massa*
recall the whole picture of an episode in the desert
when the Jewish people, wavering in faith and re-
belling against God's providence, "challenged the
Lord, and he vindicated his holiness before them"
(Num. 20:13). So it is that by constantly following
the sacred poet's analogies even the most unimagin-
ative modern mind may gradually learn to find sermons in stones, truths in the stars, and God in everything.

   That is how the Hebrew poet looks upon the world
around him. Instead of being bewitched into idolatry
by its splendor and sumptuous adornment, he has
adoration only for the divine Majesty "robed in light
as with a cloak," and spreading out the vast expanse
of the heavens like a tent cloth. All this, done by the
divine Artificer, in building His palace of the universe, raises the psalmist to such ecstasy that his

_____
[1] Knox Version.

imagination soars to the contemplation of infinite glory, even while he paints his still inadequate image:

> The clouds you make your chariot,
> you ride upon the wings of the wind.
> The storms you make your messengers,
> the fiery bolts your ministers.[1]
>
> (Ps. 103:3-4)

Even the awesome earthquake of Sinai which accompanied the great theophany, the psalmist sees under the image of the skipping and frolicking of lambs in spring (cf. Ps. 113). A superb hyperbole indeed, but poetically justified by the ecstasy of the Hebrews in their joy over the new life now opened to them as God's people. This picture ought to be a constant reminder that the delirious joy of Israel over its liberation from Egypt was but a foreshadowing of what each Christian should feel today in knowing that he too has miraculously crossed through the Red Sea, leaving his enslavement to the devil buried by Christ's redeeming death.

Also the sacred poet sees in terms of nature the first advent of the long-awaited King, "like rain coming down on the meadow" and causing the flowers of justice and of "profound peace" to bloom (Ps. 71:6-7). That, incidentally, is as near as the Israelite psalmists ever came to observing anything small in their environment. Not for them the "modest crimson-tipped flower" nor the "wee, sleeket, cowran, tim'rous beastie." Preyed upon, as they were, by

---

[1] Kleist—Lynam: The Psalms. (Bruce Publishing Co., Milwaukee, Wisc.)

powerful enemies and greedy empires, they had an eye only for the king of beasts on land or the leviathan in the sea. For in the world of their experience, force was all that counted.

The desert also had its moral teaching. For the ancient Israelite knew too well that, as a tree could thrive only in an oasis beside a flowing stream, so also man in the desert of godlessness could but wither and die for want of spiritual nourishment (Ps. 1). Likewise, the soul is compared to a water skin, which must be cared for as the very life of the desert traveler, who would not think of leaving his treasure near the fire of temptation, where it would become shriveled and useless (Ps. 118:83).

Another meaningful analogy for which many psalmists have a marked predilection is the likening of God to a *rock*, since He is the absolutely solid and unchangeable basis of Israel's hope. As the prophet Jeremias had written, "With unchanging love I love thee" (31:3), so it was the same charity, long-suffering and forever merciful, that made God the *rock* on which His people ever could find refuge. Even more: the psalmists had a vivid remembrance of the desert rock from which came the water that saved their forefathers from death (Num. 20:6-12). St. Paul tells us this rock was Christ (I Cor. 10:4). Familiar to the later psalmists, too, was the still deeper analogy of that rock seen in a dream by Nabuchodonosor, which, falling from a mountainside, destroyed all kingdoms. And then it "grew into a high mountain, filling the whole earth" (Dan. 2:35). "The prophet discerned in this stone the Messiah and his kingdom. . . . He showed Himself as stone and rock . . . to indicate that he would come in the formlessness of sinful man to re-make the earth after the pattern of his own divinity."[1]

Another kind of imagery used by the psalmists and most useful for the prayer of modern man is the depicting—under the form of God's wrath—of a divine attribute. For the making of such a picture the poet uses all the natural catastrophes due to earthquakes, thunderbolts, and roaring seas, as well as the many national disasters in Jewish history which culminated in the destruction of their temple and exile. Such phenomena and crushing misfortunes are always portrayed as the manifestations of God's intrinsic intensity and power when He fetters His love to give the world a violent reminder that "only when thy omnipotence is doubted wilt thou assert thy mastery, their rashness making manifest, who will not acknowledge thee" (Wis. 12:17). Thus any person familiar with the psalms may see in present-day calamities the wrath of God who still issues His call to order, who reminds men of their creaturely limitations, who sometimes even confounds their man-centered plans and ambitions. Especially needed nowadays is such an image of the divine anger, since the general casualness of social relations is sometimes abused by even well-meaning Christians who treat the Supreme Deity as merely "the Person upstairs." Having lost sight of the very essence of creaturehood,

---

[1] Aemilian Lohr, *The Mass Through the Year* (Westminster, Md.: The Newman Press, 1958), p. 23.

the modern world is thereby robbing the Godhead
of its utter transcendence. This means that the
foundation of worship is being undermined or entirely destroyed. It need not be so, however, since
the psalms remind one over and over that He to
whom such prayers are addressed

> . . . will crush kings on the day of his wrath.
> He will do judgment on the nations, heaping
>   up corpses;
>   he will crush heads over the wide earth.
> (Ps. 109:5-6)

Consequently, there should also be heeded the call
to

> Tremble, and serve the Lord, rejoicing in
>   his presence,
>   but with awe in your hearts.
> Kiss the rod, do not brave his anger,
>   and go astray from the sure path.
> When the fire of his vengeance blazes out
>   suddenly,
>   happy are they who find their refuge in
>   him.
> (Ps. 2:11-12)[1]

And yet, lest the vivid image of this righteous
wrath confound the hopes of mortal man, the psalmists, realizing that all attributes are but facets of
the one infinite, self-subsistent Being, have counter-
balanced the picture of an angry God by one of su-

---

[1] Knox Version.

preme love. Psalm 21 prefigures in the crucified Savior the relentless intensity of divine hatred for sin, while at the same time it portrays the all but incredible truth: "God so loved the world, that he gave up his only-begotten Son" (John 3:16).

All such imagery in the psalms should be an especial aid to the modern mind which is accustomed to concrete explanations on cinema and television. Granted that some of the word pictures used by the poet are archaic and the terms so exotic as not to be readily grasped, yet a little delving into their significance will give today's reader a depth of understanding that he never before suspected. For instance, in Psalm 1 he comes upon the image of an ancient threshing floor, which at first signifies nothing. But when he learns that in God's sight sinners are as valueless as the empty husks trampled out by oxen so as to be blown away, then he realizes as never before the instability of souls living in sin, and their fearful end.

More important than such word pictures, however, is the grand sweep of the psalmist's canvas as he paints in living colors the whole panorama of man's moral warfare. For what else are those bloody battlefields with all their carnage but an enlargement of each individual's struggle to fight his way home to God over the corpses of his passions and evil tendencies? That is why someone has said that the psalms are forerunners of the great spiritual autobiographies. They do indeed dramatize in unforgettable terms the futile efforts of the sinner sunk in the morass of overwhelming temptations, until he can say with a thankful heart:

Resplendent you came, O powerful One,
from the everlasting mountains. . . .
At your rebuke, O God of Jacob,
chariots and steeds lay stilled.

(Ps. 75:5, 7)

Yet, despite all that has been said, it still remains true that the modern mind, trained to reason scientifically from cause to effect, is necessarily baffled at first by the psalmist's use of analogies between the material world and things spiritual, by this effort to extract a religious meaning from within the physical reality. But what Daniélou quotes Jung as saying concerning pagan myths applies with even more validity to the analogies found in the psalms: " . . . they are the expression of the deepest psychological reality; . . . they belong to the structure of the soul itself."[1] Moreover, one can read in the Psalter the whole story of God's marvelous acts, His revelation of Himself to man: first in nature, then through the historical events by which He prepared His people for truths surpassing all natural knowledge, until that "hour" when the Word itself was made flesh and told in human language "the wonderful works of God" (Acts 2:11).[2]

Finally, the psalms, which teach man not only to pray but at the same time to receive the Word into his innermost heart, are a form of theology in action, a knowing that terminates in doing. For they are a contemplation of the living God expressed in a form

---

[1] Quoted by Daniélou, *op. cit.*, p. 134.

[2] Douay Version.

most suited to man's dual nature: they manifest in terms perceivable by the senses all the mighty works in space and time that tell His glory. He it is whose infinite beauty, reflected everywhere in the natural and spiritual spheres, has ever impelled man to pay Him fitting homage in the tribute of the highest possible art—in sculpture, painting, music, architecture, and also in poetry.

Part Two

MEDITATING THE PSALMS

FIRST STEP

PSALMS FOR THE PRESSURES OF MODERN LIFE

This first step takes up the particular psalms that help to deal with the problems arising in everyday life. These psalms may be used as a kind of fore-Mass, i.e., a preparation, to give one's life a whole new dimension for taking part with Christ in the great mysteries contained in the psalms to follow.

Psalm 1—Where Happiness Is Found in the World Today

In this ancient hymn, filled though it is with pictures of oriental life, the psalmist conveys a surprisingly vivid impression of the world today, with all its spiritual hazards, deceptions, and finally its age-old secret of true happiness.

But first the negative side: how not to be happy in this world where we are bombarded on all sides by countless devices pressuring our desires, until we feel impelled to think of life solely in terms of possessing at any cost the means to pleasure, profit, or power. If we resist such a temptation, we may yet find ourselves bogged down in triviality and futility by having heeded that *counsel of the wicked*: "It's smart to play it safe. No use being a hero if you are dead!" Or else we poor moderns may fall prey to cynics, the *insolent* of our day, who pessimistically advise us "not really to care about anything, and you'll not get hurt." How many persons find themselves thus drained of all spontaneity and enthusiasm, which give zest and happiness to living? With life emptied of real depth and significance, they try to fill the vacuum with constant meaningless activity, noise, and excitement. But then they only increase the disorder, artificiality, and hollowness of a soul that none but God can fill.

> Happy the man who follows not
>   the counsel of the wicked
> Nor walks in the way of sinners,
>   nor sits in the company of the insolent.

The way to find true happiness, on the other hand, is to transform the passionate desire of possessing into an equally great longing to be possessed. The means of accomplishing this is to *meditate* on *the law of the Lord*. Here, it must be hastily noted, *law* is far more than the technical term for that burden of legalism which moderns especially find repugnant. The psalmist uses the word *law* to mean the whole of God's beautiful revelation concentrated like a radiant beam of truth on the short book of the Psalter. To meditate on the *law*, then, would be to commune with God through assiduously using the psalms in order to learn and assimilate the divine thoughts until they become part and fiber of one's own being.

Yet, even so, meditation is a forbidding word to modern man with his restless heart and his undisciplined mind that is fed on the intellectual pablum of run-of-the-mill cinema or television entertainment. Consequently for him a most timely introduction to this all-important spiritual exercise is the psalms. This is because they were composed according to the ancient Hebrew manner of meditating, not by silent concentration but by a repetitious murmuring of sacred words and phrases, until these are woven spontaneously into the very texture of one's thought and speech. This, of course, would be an excellent beginning of meditation for any sincere Christian in the modern world, where everything is designed to keep his mind from reflecting. His next step would consist in striving to attain such unity of his mental and spiritual powers as will help surmount distractions. Therefore, especially when praying the psalms, he will endeavor to relax, to be still in desire and thought, so as to let God's dynamic truth seep through a selfless absorption in divine reality. For meditation on the law begins with an attitude of mind set by the will, which places one's whole being at the disposition of an all-loving Father in total response to His revealed Word.

In addition, the psalmist shrewdly mentions *delights* as a further attraction for his recipe on how to be happy here and now. Thereby he seems uncannily to prophesy the distinguishing mark of our generation: boredom. This may be the sensual satiety afflicting secular life, or it may be the spiritual ennui of the last few centuries, when hungry souls were given the insufficient food of man-made "devotions"

dished up without variety day after day and lacking
the dynamic stimulation of the inspired Word. Here
the poet speaks for all times when he gives the
assurance that God's law, or self-revelation, is so
brimming over with inexhaustible vitality and new
discoveries that every psalm—even every re-reading
of a familiar psalm—means the disclosure of fresh
and capitivating truths that always delight the heart
but never fill the mind to satiety.

> But delights in the law of the Lord
>   and meditates on his law day and night.

Like the sacraments God's *law* is spiritual-corporal:
it works in man of flesh and blood, nourishing his
spirit unto power in his life and actions. To use the
desert simile, he is *like a tree planted near* the *run-
ning water* of divine grace, which enables him always
to bear the fruit of virtues and good works. For, as
St. James explains in his epistle, "You are to live by
the word, not content merely to listen to it. . . .
Whereas one who gazes into that perfect law . . .
and dwells on the sight of it, does not forget its message; he finds something to do and does it" (1:22,
25).

> He is like a tree
>   planted near running water,
> That yields its fruit in due season,
>   and whose leaves never fade.
> Whatever he does prospers.

Christians today, however, must do even more
than put forth leaves and fruits; they must be even as
their Head, the great Protagonist struggling with the

Powers of Darkness. That is, members of Christ may not withdraw in contempt or despair from a world without basic principles, tossed to and fro by fear and vain desires. They must give themselves in love, sympathy, and understanding to those who lack the time—even the will—to listen because their thoughts are scattered in all directions, fretting about family, friends, enemies, work, or ambitions. Yet the lay apostle, failing to win his fellow men, must also take care not to fall prey to the endemic disease of activism, from which too many would-be Catholic actionists in America are apt to suffer. Therefore, the psalmist here reiterates his emphasis on the imperative need for a mind disciplined by meditation amid the frenzied restlessness and disorder everywhere today. As object lesson he singles out the devotees of pleasure, comparing them to *chaff*, light enough to be carried about on every breeze of a new sensation.

> Not so the wicked, not so;
>> they are like chaff which the wind drives
>> away.

As if that warning were still not enough, the poet ends by contrasting the final destinies of the good and the wicked of any era, when they meet at God's judgment seat. There without advocate, *sinners* who made this world their total aim will try to hide from the face of long-spurned truth. The *just,* on the contrary, who always strove to make God the goal of their hearts' desires, will have the whole communion of saints to plead their cause. Thus the faithful under divine protection will enter into eternal happiness, while the wicked will have learned at last that their

smooth expressway of reckless pleasure has but one
end—the pit of endless woe.

> Therefore in judgment the wicked shall not
>   stand,
>   nor shall sinners, in the assembly of the
>   just.
> For the Lord watches over the way of the
>   just,
>   but the way of the wicked vanishes.

Psalm 18—God's Two Meditation Books

A-I

Prayer that comes from the heart often begins with
the discovery of nature as God's handiwork. Through
nature He reveals Himself to anyone who will pause
and heed the wondrous message. More than ever, in
this era of unprecedented scientific probing into the
cosmic mysteries, how plainly the stupendous power
locked in the smallest atom, the as-yet unattainable
reaches of interstellar space, or the unexplored potentialities in the sun—all tell the wisdom, the infinite
intelligence, the awe-inspiring majesty of their Creator. As the whole vast universe is charged with
mysterious physical forces emanating from solar
energy, so likewise is the spiritual world continually
vibrating with the Sun of the divine Word, the Source
of all creation. Moreover, this Word, besides being a
creative power, is also a message that permeates,
warms and enlightens, as does the sun.

Such is the silent message of all creation. Yet how
can persons in the modern world hear the voices of

nature, as did Wordsworth when he wrote, "In the mountains did he feel his faith"? For most people today live in cities, where we have smothered in solid concrete the good and fruitful earth, and have reduced the heavens to murky silence with our smog. Therefore, God has inspired this psalm, as if made especially for the modern Christian, to help fill up the man-made deficit of artificiality by revealing how everything—planet, hill, and tree—proclaims from the depth of its being the joy and goodness and beauty of its Maker.

> The heavens declare the glory of God,
>> and the firmament proclaims his handi-
>> work.
> Day pours out the word to day,
>> and night to night imparts knowledge;
> Not a word nor a discourse
>> whose voice is not heard;
> Through all the earth their voice resounds,
>> and to the ends of the world, their mes-
>> sage.

II

Above all, the sun—which modern man is wont to take for granted, though the ancients worshipped it in wonder—brings to earth God's wordless message. How this champion of immeasurable energy, parting the gorgeous tapestries of dawn, goes forth in all his power and majesty, the image of God Himself, who with His vivifying love ever passes through creation, awakening it to light and life.

He has pitched a tent there for the sun,
  which comes forth like the groom from
    his bridal chamber
  and, like a giant, joyfully runs its course.
At one end of the heavens it comes forth,
  and its course is to their other end;
  nothing escapes its heat.

B-I

What the sun does for the earth that also the Word accomplishes for souls. The necessary contact is effected when any person recognizes that the Word, which speaks from out the Bible today as always, is actually the Lord God, not only guiding by His precepts but also drawing all hearts by revealing to them His inmost nature and personality. Thus a man will realize that the divine *law* is really a living Word not engraved on tablets of stone but in the flesh of the human heart. And since that same Word is ever creative, through its abiding message it forms into new men all who surrender themselves to its renewing power.

How far the law is from being a dead letter or an uninspired legalism the psalmist proves by communicating the experience of his faith in the form of a "litany of the divine word" fervently invoked under every name given it by the People of God: *law, precepts, commands, fear,* and *ordinances.* All of these terms but denote the Christian's right attitude of being ever at the disposition of his Lord.

By its parallelism Hebrew poetry helps the reader to examine the law as if it were a jewel, holding it at various angles so that he may be completely captivated by its total beauty. In this way the psalm reveals the law as a refreshing drink when the soul is famishing for truth; or else as a lamp of learning for any who are simple enough to seek wisdom. Again, the inspired word uses every incentive to attract men ever deeper into sacred intimacy. So the *rejoicing* of *the heart*, attained by meditating on the law, is a reflection of the bond uniting the supreme Deity with His lowly creature. This joy is also a lure to draw man on to ever new discoveries in the glory that surrounds him and into which he plunges ever more deeply through his meditations.

> The law of the Lord is perfect,
>> refreshing the soul;
> The decree of the Lord is trustworthy,
>> giving wisdom to the simple.
> The precepts of the Lord are right,
>> rejoicing the heart;
> The command of the Lord is clear,
>> enlightening the eye;
> The fear of the Lord is pure,
>> enduring forever;
> The ordinances of the Lord are true,
>> all of them just;
> They are more precious than gold;
>> than a heap of purest gold;
> Sweeter also than syrup
>> or honey from the comb.

II

With mind thus focussed on the law and filled with a vivid sense of the divine Word, whoever medi-

tates with a living faith hears the spoken Word just
as the prophets did, only not in the same manner.
And if a soul cooperates with grace, there is bound
to be a progressive deepening of spiritual insight and
a consequent enrichment of its inner life. Moreover,
since this prayer of faith is an interchange between
the Word and man, made possible through the
psalms, there must be a divinely activated response
on the part of him who has so meditated. The following verses show what that response ought to be.

First, there will be found a fear of offending God,
even inadvertently.

> Though your servant is careful of them,
>   very diligent in keeping them,
> Yet who can detect failings?
> Cleanse me from my unknown faults!

Then the soul will be especially alert to guard
against the very root of evil, which is pride.[1] This
capital sin could make any man on earth take his
Godlike intellect and cast it into infernal darkness
with the cry of Lucifer, "I will not serve!"

> From wanton sin especially, restrain your
>   servant;
>   let it not rule over me.

---

[1] Thus Boylan and Kissane interpret the "wanton sin" as referring
to that of the proud, "sins committed with a high hand" (Kissane:
The Book of Psalms, vol. 1, Newman, Westminster, Md., p. 87).
Fillion, however, construes the expression as indicating "formal
apostasy" (*The New Book of the Roman Breviary*, M. Louis, Herder,
4th ed., 1932, p. 132n).

Then shall I be blameless and innocent
    of serious sin.

But those who have utterly surrendered to the
divine will are led by the Spirit, who conducts them
through the law to the other side. Here may be found
the inner substance of that law, where it is no longer
seen from without but from within. And here it is
found to be not law but love.

Let the words of my mouth
    and the thought of my heart find favor
        before you,
O Lord, my rock and my redeemer.

Psalm 8—Nature Reveals the Imprint of God's Hands

Meditation on this beautiful psalm can restore to
modern man something very valuable in the texture
of his thinking—namely, a reverential attitude toward
all creation, together with a new and vital realization
of his own place in it. For the psalmist shows the
paramount importance for everyone sometimes to
stop and ponder, observing with care his natural
surroundings, not with the cold, calculating eye of an
efficiency expert, but with the loving awareness of
an adorer. For all these things are radiant with the imprint of God's hands. In this age, however, when the
fascination for applied science has largely smothered
the poetic faculty, most people tend to see only the
objective facts of natural phenomena, instead of being filled with a sense of adoring wonder. Yet such
a vision would have but one effect: it would elevate

to a new spiritual level of existence all who could discern in creation a reflection of the intelligence and love which called it into being.

Through this psalm one may also perceive, amid all the complexities of the vast universe, that everything is in its divinely assigned place. For the *name* of God—i.e., His personal revelation transmitted by His Word, has shown the meaning and order in everything. To apprehend all this can give one's life a depth and fulness of significance that were not there before. Thus it will be found that all created things— from the moon to the lowliest insect—have their own special glory. Each serves as God's instrument in leading those who study it from the meaningless morass of our materialistic culture up to the sunlit heights of belief in the infinite intelligence. Thereupon reason itself will demand that the soul bow down in awe at God's wisdom traced so plainly in the shadowy reflection of His handiwork.

> O Lord, our Lord,
>> how glorious is your name over all the
>> earth!
>> You have exalted your majesty above the
>> heavens.

The Savior Himself once quoted the next verse of this psalm when the worldly-wise rulers of the Jews, having closed their minds to the proofs of His messiahship, remonstrated that the children in the temple were proclaiming His praises. Jesus reminded them that God Himself inspires such fitting homage wherever He finds souls still alight with the pene-

trating vision of childlike innocence and detachment
from the sordid machinations of this world.

> Out of the mouths of babes and sucklings
>   you have fashioned praise because of
>   your foes,
>   to silence the hostile and the vengeful.

It has often been said that no true astronomer
is an atheist. How could he be when he studies the
masses of the planets and the inconceivable immensity of interstellar space? Also, how could he fail
to be humbled at perceiving the contrast between the
majestic vastness of the heavens and the insignifi-
cance called man? Well should anyone wonder that
the Omnipotence which made and governs the huge
and spacious universe should deign to notice the
tiny atom of mere humanity.

> When I behold your heavens, the work of
>   your fingers,
>   the moon and the stars which you set in
>   place—(I wonder)
> What is man that you should be mindful
>   of him,
>   or the son of man that you should care
>   for him?

II

Only through revelation, then, could humanity
ever have come to believe in its own importance.
Only God could have made known His incompre-
hensible love in creating man to His own image,

while at the same time making him "less than the angels." That is, although man is crowned with the godlike attributes of intelligence and free will, he is nevertheless bound to time and space, as well as encumbered with a body subject to the vicissitudes of sickness, weariness, and death.

> You have made him little less than the
>   angels,
> and crowned him with glory and honor.

Every person, moreover, even the meanest beggar, is God's regent on earth, placed here by gift of His sovereign majesty and endowed with an inalienable right to the enjoyment and ownership of its goods. The only condition is that he use these things as God means them to be used, reverently lifting them up as a sacrifice of praise while thanking the Lord for all the wisdom and goodness and bounty which have bestowed them.

> You have given him rule over the works of
>   your hands,
>   putting all things under his feet:
> All sheep and oxen,
>   yes, and the beasts of the field,
> The birds of the air, the fishes of the sea,
>   and whatever swims the paths of the
>   seas.

This means, then, that the Christian must learn to view the world around him with heart as well as with eyes. It means loving things for what they are in themselves, as God's creatures, apart from their practical usefulness in daily living. It means penetrating beyond the reality of what one sees and feels and touches to the far greater Reality that reveals itself only to those who search in earnest and ponder what they find. For all creation, if contemplated with reverence, can give an intimation of the infinite horizons which lie beyond the reaches of our finite intellect.

> Oh Lord, our Lord,
>> how glorious is your name over all the earth!

Thus this short psalm can lead the thoughtful mind back to its primary purpose of wonder—even to a far-off vision of the God whose marvelous attributes it will be man's privilege to contemplate in an eternal sharing of His own intimate and triune life. The child, St. Thérèse, well expressed such a discovery of the Creator after viewing the overwhelming majesty of the Alps. "This scenery will give me courage," she wrote. "I shall no longer attach any importance to my petty concerns when I think of the power and grandeur of God."[1] She too had acquired the wisdom not of this world from contemplating in nature's marvels the imprint of His hands.

Psalm 120—Divine Insurance for Life's Pilgrimage

This psalm offers the reader a good way to pause and check his route in the midst of his pilgrimage to eternity. Few would deny how necessary it is for one to stop now and then amid the humdrum grind of daily duties and make sure he is still on course. Just as

[1] Hans Urs von Balthazar, *Thérèse of Lisieux* (New York, Sheed and Ward, 1954), p. 130.

the navigator ordinarily steers by the stars, the Christian can raise his mental gaze to the far-off *mountains* of that eternal abode, which is not only his ultimate destination but the source of all his power to attain it.

> I lift up my eyes toward the mountains;
>   whence shall help come to me?
> My help is from the Lord,
>   who made heaven and earth.

One may recall how once on the Sea of Galilee the apostles, with Christ asleep in the storm-tossed boat, doubted His watchful care. How often souls today, buffeted by the savage waves of some adversity, have thought, too, that the Lord was sleeping. Their cry for help seemed to go unheard. But in this next verse they, like the apostles, can hear again the Savior's own assurance of constant watchfulness: "Why are you fainthearted, men of little faith?"

> May he not suffer your foot to slip;
>   may he slumber not who guards you:
> Indeed he neither slumbers nor sleeps,
>   the guardian of Israel.

Modern self-sufficiency often tends to relegate God to being "on call" only in cases of emergency. In everyday affairs help from the Lord is too frequently regarded as divine interference in a world that belongs exclusively to men. Yet to such a pagan attitude how the following verse gives the lie, proclaiming as it does that the Good Shepherd never ceases His solicitude for His creatures.

The Lord is your guardian; the Lord is your
    shade;
he is beside you at your right hand.

The significance of that last line must not be lost
in this age of automatic weapons. In ancient battle
a soldier carried his shield in his left hand, thereby
exposing his right side to attack. This verse implies
that, if one uses to the full the shield of his personal
efforts, then his *right hand*—where human limitations
fail—will be defended by God's own power.

Not only in the actual fight against temptation
but also in every circumstance of life, the modern
Christian too can rely upon this divine protection.
Although he may be exposed to the glare of public
acclaim, the *sun* of success need not harm him. Nor
on the other hand, will he suffer damage from the
cold rays of the *moon*. This could mean the "dark
night of the soul," when God temporarily withdraws
His consolations. He does this only to let souls find
out if they are really seeking Him or only looking for
their own interests when they pray.

The sun shall not harm you by day,
    nor the moon by night.

The last two verses are like a divine insurance
policy especially drawn up to cover the hazards of
modern living. For everyone knows that sudden death
of soul or body lurks in many places along life's high-
way. The following words, then, can help Christians
to be confident in all eventualities with this assurance: no matter where you are or in what danger
you find yourself—

> The Lord will guard you from all evil;
>   he will guard your life.
> The Lord will guard your coming and your
>   going,
>   both now and forever.

Psalm 123—Without God Life Would Be Too Perilous

This psalm offers the Christian in the world today some divinely inspired encouragement for his daily struggle. That is, the implied note of thankfulness suggests that the Lord was with the psalmist, who has come safely through all perils—so far!

> Had not the Lord been with us,
>   let Israel [my soul] say,
>   had not the Lord been with us—

What else could the first of those deadly dangers be for us but the very atmosphere in which we live and breathe: that gross self-indulgence which permeates much of what we see and hear and read that we unconsciously absorb its false values into the very texture of our thinking? For example, who has not at some time or other yielded, at least in thought, to the lure of the so-called "good life"; that is, a life filled with purposeless leisure and self-gratification? Or who of us has never once found himself entertaining the subtle suggestion of certain authors and playwrights that the only reasonable solution to some given problem is that which will bring a pseudo-happiness here and now? With all this in mind, one may find the following verses quite apropos to modern life and also a solemn warning to be ever on the alert.

When men rose up against us
   [with the philosophy that pleasure is the
       only good],
   then would they have swallowed us alive.
When their fury was inflamed against us
   [in our striving for real Christian values],
   then would the waters [of temptation]
   have overwhelmed us.

Thus weakened by the poisonous atmosphere exhaled from this cult of self-indulgence, we are all constantly assailed by a veritable tidal wave of high-powered advertisements pressuring us on all sides. Amassing all the forces of human motives from fear to concupiscence, that mighty torrent bears down upon a person's reason in order to press beyond his means for the things he does not need nor would otherwise even desire. But who can long withstand the specter of social ostracism held out as the only alternative to adopting the "latest," the "newest," the "most revolutionary" . . .? Who indeed—*had not the Lord been with us* to bolster our resistance by His gospel reminder, "Blessed are the poor in spirit; the kingdom of heaven is theirs" (Matt. 5:3)?

Only with this beatitude in mind can one learn to use all material possessions—luxuries or necessities—as gifts from God and therefore to be owned and enjoyed within the framework of His providence. Thus a Christian would not be tempted to covet things for sensual pleasure or for their prestige value. He could, on the contrary, come to look upon all modern conveniences that are lawful as true love tokens from a bountiful Creator offered in due measure to ease this earthly pilgrimage and quest for our eternal home. Aided then by the spirit of this beatitude, he may say this next verse in heartfelt gratitude that the Lord has been on our side with His saving grace and truth.

> The torrent would have swept over us;
>   over us then would have swept
>   the raging waters.
> Blessed be the Lord, who did not leave us
>   a prey to their teeth.

Although a person may have emerged from one siege of temptation, he still can never relax as if out of danger. So long as we are living in this world we are always in peril of becoming enmeshed in its allurements. The demands of life and our changing social conventions tend to weave a net that renders captive our wills, making us as helpless as a *bird* caught in a *snare*. God alone has sufficient might to break this web of ingrained habits and tendencies. He alone can set our soul free, provided it has the will to escape into the liberty of the sons of God.

> We were rescued like a bird
>   from the fowler's snare;
> Broken was the snare,
>   and we were freed.

So powerful does the Church consider the next inspired truth that she has embedded this verse in her daily Mass and Divine Office. Nor could one seek any better recommendation for using it as a frequent ejaculation throughout the day, both as a divine aid and a reminder:

> Our help is in the name of the Lord,
> who made heaven and earth.

Psalm 92—Only in God Can the Soul Today Stand Sure

In this present cold war of nerves most of us are living in some fear of communism and its incredible success in devising weapons for men's subjugation. When we read of the Soviet Union's ruthless terrorism over captive nations, its clever penetration into new territories, its tireless scheming, and now its intercontinental ballistic missile, we may sometimes be tempted to doubt, perhaps subconsciously, the reality of that Power which really holds in leash all the forces of evil. So it is quite salutary that the Christian today place himself often amid the imagery of this divinely inspired psalm where—

> The Lord is king, in splendor robed;
>   robed is the Lord and girt about with
>   strength;
> And he has made the world firm,
>   not to be moved.

To feel the full force of such unshakeable trust in Omnipotence over the affairs of time, Christians today should first glimpse the meaning of His eternity. Then they shall better understand that—ephemeral creatures though we are, fearful of the present and ignorant of the morrow—we are not helpless victims of man's unbridled bestiality. There is a part of us that no evil power can ever touch without our consent, since through sharing in the divine life we

are even now in spirit within the serene abode of
God's eternal present. From there we can recognize
that infinite Wisdom even nowadays disposes all
things mightily. For He is unerringly bent on the
fulfilment of His plan of love made before ever the
world was formed.

> Your throne stands firm from of old;
>   from everlasting you are, O Lord.

With such truths in mind, one who prays this psalm
may bolster his trust even more by scanning the les-
sons of history. How many powerful movements of
nations or ideologies were once like torrential *floods*
sweeping away whole civilizations and undermining
the very foundations of Christian culture. Such were
the barbarian invasions of Europe, the Moslem in-
cursions against the Middle East, and the Protestant
Revolt. Such also is the Communist movement today,
which threatens to end our civilization, on which
many now vainly base their whole sense of security.
Yet, though inundating whole continents for long
centuries at a time, none of those destructive forces
has ever succeeded in obliterating Christianity. We
know they cannot do so because they are beating
against the rock of an Omnipotence that nothing can
ever dislodge.

> The floods lift up, O Lord,
>   the floods lift up their voice;
>   the floods lift up their tumult.

A survey of today's world will reveal a chaotic
sea of moral bankruptcy and bewilderment, which
threatens even more ominously to engulf our present

way of life and sweep the whole world into a new and more horrible abyss of "Dark Ages." For instance, we Americans have more statutes on the books than any other nation, yet we are being drowned in an ocean of lawlessness. The philosophies taught in our schools have made a shambles of the Ten Commandments, while some of our very "educators" proclaim any certainty to be a myth. Although we live amid the greatest material luxury ever known, we are nevertheless squandering our natural resources in the flimsy belief that safety lies solely in hydrogen bombs and intercontinental missiles. While making mutual defense coalitions with East and West, we seem to ignore the one coalition that can actually keep us from being instantly obliterated. That is a treaty, not of lip service but of sincere allegiance to the principles of the One who holds absolute sway over all the schemes and forces of men.

> More powerful than the roar of many
>   waters,
>   more powerful than the breakers of the
>   sea—
>   powerful on high is the Lord.

This has been well called the age of "the big lie," since that device has toppled nations into the maw of communism. But this is also the age of the little lie, which ranges all the way from fibs of social convenience down to formal perjury—almost a commonplace in our courts nowadays. Where then shall anybody find faith on earth except in Him who is the only one that ever claimed to be the Truth?

Your decrees are worthy of trust indeed.

Where are those *decrees* to be found with certainty? In the Church, the guardian of Scripture and the *house* of the Lord, where abides that holiness which is utterly incompatible with any falsehood or deception. Despite the inevitable lack of integrity in many of those who dwell therein, Christians know that the Church is nevertheless impregnated with God's own intrinsic and indestructible sanctity. So this is where they may always secure their own faith on a firm foundation, exclaiming with the psalmist:

> Holiness befits your house,
> O Lord, for length of days.

That is, until the walls of this world have crumbled to reveal the ever-abiding fortress of God's eternal truth and omnipotence.

Psalm 121—The Church as Viewed From Within

This psalm gives him who reads with insight a most inspiring spiritual view of the Church depicted in all its beauty as both the City of man's desires and the Body of Christ living on earth today. Anyone who has faith in both these aspects can exclaim with all sincerity:

> I rejoiced because they said to me,
> "We will go up to the house of the Lord."

Just what is this *house*, praised so ecstatically by the psalmist as the longed-for goal of life's journey? It is the world-encompassing City of God, in which

Christians find themselves incorporated through baptism.

> And now we have set foot
> within your gates, O Jerusalem—

Moreover, St. Peter describes the Church under the figure of a vast cathedral constructed of living stones that are cemented together by the unifying force of the divine life (I Pet. 2:4):

> Jerusalem, built as a city
> with compact unity.

The Church, however, is not like a material structure, since this takes its form from the shape and character of its stones. Nor does she forge human beings into a rigid mass of standardized parts. On the contrary, she preserves every man's unique personality even while moulding each and all to the pattern of Christ. And all the while they, no longer isolated and helpless individuals, are associated with the aid and merits of those who have already been tried and found worthy, the apostles and the saints. With their aid and in their company, he who prays this psalm may consciously unite himself to the living body of Christ, whose chief purpose for remaining on earth is to pay fitting honor to the infinite majesty of the Godhead.

> To it the tribes go up,
> the tribes of the Lord,
> According to the decree for Israel,
> to give thanks to the name of the Lord.

In it are set up judgment seats [for the
    apostles],
  seats for the house of David [Christ].

As Christians pray this psalm, then, they find themselves acting in unison with that great assemblage
of heaven and earth. Can they, under such circumstances, confine their petitions to mere personal
trifles? Or should they not rather

Pray for the peace of Jerusalem [the
    Church]?

This means to ask that her members on earth may
realize how unthinkable are personal hatreds and
rivalries among those actually joined together by
the strongest possible bond, their common life in
Christ.

May those who love you prosper!
May peace be within your walls,
  prosperity in your buildings.
Because of my relatives and friends
  I will say, "Peace be within you!"
Because of the house of the Lord, our God,
  I will pray for your good.

All this is how the Church should appear, how she
functions, if viewed not superficially with the critical
gaze of natural and worldly values, but with the penetrating eye of a supernatural faith. So all Catholics
should recognize throughout this world-wide organism a common unity and aim, however these may be
encrusted by human weakness or thwarted by the
cross-purposes of men. For "we, though many in

number, form one body in Christ" (Rom. 12:5), and
the life that animates the whole is divine.

Psalm 86—A Prayer That Is Catholic in Its Universality

Almost everyone today is sufficiently imbued with
the individualism of the age to have acquired an
inclination to think about life's purpose in terms of
"saving my own soul." This is all well and good. But
Psalm 86 will help preserve the right balance between such an individualistic mentality and catholicity (with a small *c*). For this poem clearly makes
known that the special object of God's love is not the
single soul, as such, but the Church, since she is the
very Body of His beloved Son. Individuals are really
lovable only in so far as they are incorporated in—
identified with—Christ.

> His foundation upon the holy mountains
>   the Lord loves:
> The gates of Sion,
>   more than any dwelling of Jacob.

One of the most remarkable things about the
Church is her all-inclusive catholicity. And this term
means more than her embracing in membership
types of mankind from every race and nation. It
means more even than her extraordinary power of
accommodating to one formula of faith men of diverse
cultures. Catholicity is a divine alchemy that enables
the Church to absorb any people's local customs and
culture so as to transmute them into something of
an eternal value. See how she has already done this
with the art and architecture of the Orient, and even

with some of the music from Africa. To this end the Church possesses a supernatural dynamism that enables her to penetrate everything not intrinsically evil in order to bring not only all souls but all creation under the headship of Christ.

> Glorious things are said of you,
> O city of God!

Next, one may observe how all-inclusive is that catholicity which embraces in this prayer for conversion even erstwhile enemies like the *Egypt* and *Babylon* of our day—i.e., Russia and China. Other nations, too, are easily identifiable. For the inhabitants of *Philistia* can be substituted the Moslems, who are also irreconcilable foes of God's people. In the Tyrians, those merchants of the ancient world, the reader may pray for all individuals of any land who are so bent on worldly gain as to lose sight of the priceless pearl of faith.

The people of *Ethiopia* should be a timely reminder that the Negro also is entitled to a place in our midst—and not with condescension on our part. For his race, with its native gift for melody and expressive rhythm, may well enrich the Church with a new and colorful Christian culture, which some day could even be embodied in the liturgy.

> I tell of Egypt and Babylon
> among those that know the Lord;
> Of Philistia, Tyre, Ethiopia:
> "This man was born there [in the
> Church]."

The conversion of all nations, for which the psalm thus prays, has one most remarkable feature, which

the United States naturalization laws cannot dupli-
cate. Within the Church each person is truly born
again, completely transformed into a new man, sharing the divine life and possessing as a birthright all
the powers and privileges of full citizenship in the
heavenly kingdom.

> And of Sion they shall say:
>   "One and all were born in her;
> And he who has established her
>   is the Most High Lord."

All this surely ought to make one pause and think
how utterly inconsistent is any kind of exclusiveness,
especially among Catholics. St. Paul long ago pointed
out that in Christ's Mystical Body there is a recipro-
cal dependence between the lowly feet and the
lordly eye (I Cor. 12:12-26). Moreover, in the final
analysis all Christians are spiritual refugees from
unredemption, admitted without any merit of theirs
to share in the divine life gratuitously distributed to
every one, regardless of race, economic status, or
color.

> They shall note, when the peoples are en-
>   rolled:
>   "This man was born there."
> And all shall sing, in their festive dance:
>   "My home is within you."

Psalm 47—Knowledge in Depth for an Apostolate

I

The Church is truly so wonderful that its members
should in all charity and generosity seek to share it

with others. Psalm 47 will help them to do so, since
this is a meditative poem that points out some of the
soul-satisfying aspects of the Church. For instance,
it is the *city* where God Himself dwells surrounded
on high by creatures of grace who are lost in the
abyss of their wonder at His fathomless beauty. It
is also a *holy mountain* bathed in the sunlight of
divine love, while at the same time it is a strong
fortress which, forbidding only to its enemies, is to
those who dwell therein the *joy of all the earth.* From
the New Testament, too, Christians know that the
Church is a divine and living organism, radiant with
inner beauty and imbued with a vital force, since
it is the Body of Christ-on-earth and therefore ani-
mated by His glorious risen life. That final revelation
seems to have been glimpsed also by the ancient
prophet when he sang this hymn of praise.

> Great is the Lord and wholly to be praised
>   in the city of our God.
> His holy mountain, fairest of heights,
>   is the joy of all the earth;
> Mount Sion, "the recesses of the North,"[1]
>   is the city of the great King.
> God is with her castles;
>   renowned is he as a stronghold.

II

> For lo! the kings assemble,
>   they come on together;

---

[1] A traditional name for the earthly abode of God.

They also see, and at once are stunned,
    terrified, routed.

Well has history borne out this fact—from Julian
the Apostate's despairing cry, "Thou hast conquered,
Galilean!" to Hitler's frenzied boast that he would
"bury the corpse of Catholicism" beneath the mound
of his conquests. Yet there have been many others
suddenly converted to Christ, like St. Paul on the
Damascus road or Claudel at a Christmas midnight
Mass. These men were so overwhelmed at God's sudden counterattack that they surrendered unconditionally, as soon as they realized the Omnipotence
they had challenged in the rash lustihood of their
young defiance.

Quaking seizes them there;
    anguish, like a woman's in labor.

For each individual must have first been drawn by
divine love into the Church's maternal womb, so as to
be reborn a child of God.

As though a wind from the east
    were shattering ships of Tharsis.

That is to say, such complete conversions mean the
shattering of all worldly schemes and ambitions,
which the Almighty has demolished with a blow. But
in the case of souls shipwrecked on divine mercy,
God does not destroy those who surrender. Instead,
He overwhelms them with love, saying: "All that I
took from thee I did but take/ not for thy harms,
/but just that thou might'st seek it in my arms. . . .
/Rise, clasp my hand and come."

III

The following stanza could well be some recent convert's song of ecstatic thankfulness that the Church has truly lived up to all his expectations. Yet there are many conversions or turning points in every Godward-directed life, including that of a "cradle Catholic." How many times already he may have rounded the corner of some fresh discovery about his faith, only to come upon an unexpected vista of overwhelming beauty. If, however, anyone has at other times found his appreciation worn thin by long taking-for-granted, he could read these next verses thoughtfully in conscious effort to realize anew the wonders of this *city* and of his deliverance, through the Church, from the exile of unredemption.

> As we had heard, so have we seen
> in the city of the Lord of hosts,
> In the city of our God;
> God makes it firm forever.
> O God, we ponder your kindness
> within your temple.
> As your name, O God, so also your praise
> reaches to the ends of the earth.
> Of justice your right hand is full;
> let Mount Sion be glad,
> Let the cities of Juda rejoice,
> because of your judgments.

If, however, any one should find this prayer too ecstatic for his current state of mind, it may be that he needs a closer knowledge in depth of his faith. This can be acquired by reading widely and wisely books that portray the Church in all her dynamic beauty as Christ's own Mystical Body on earth. Such reading will indeed enable one to

> Go about Sion, make the round;
>   count her towers [of resplendent truths],
> Consider her ramparts,
>   examine her castles.

Those *ramparts* could stand for the Church's social doctrine, embedded in the very nature of human society and of far-reaching spiritual significance. For instance, human dignity and family or community integrity, which are always morally inviolable. Also such concepts as the all-embracing fatherhood of God. These are important strongholds of such spiritual insight into the faith as will be needed for any apostolate, whether it be to those outside the fold or to one's own fellow Catholics, whom he may endeavor to awaken to a whole new world of discovery. For there is always this about learning each new aspect of God's truth: it brings with it an inward compulsion

> That you may tell a future generation
>   that such is God,
> Our God forever and ever;
>   he will guide us.

Psalm 147—God's Providence Is as Sure as Nature's Laws

This exquisite psalm may first be read purely as a nature poem, for the cadence of the lines and their inherent vitality. Then above this marvelous pulsation of natural phenomena, in His unchanging eternity, is found God, who controls and directs every detail by the mere breath of His will. In this manner the psalm portrays all of nature as an unceasing hymn of praise to its Maker, because it is subservient to His slightest wish. Man too may join this cosmic chorus, first by sometimes pausing to admire nature's wondrous works, and then by using his mind and will to "magnify the Lord."

Besides the literal meaning, however, this psalm also has a deep spiritual significance. For it praises the Lord of Creation not only through His material works of wonder, but also through the greatest of His spiritual achievements, the Church, that new and heavenly Jerusalem.

> Glorify the Lord, O Jerusalem;
> praise your God, O Sion.

How marvelously the Lord has constructed this living temple of His worship on earth! He has protected it from contamination of error and defilement by bolting fast with infallibility the *gates* of its doctrine and moral teaching. Those who dwell therein He *has blessed* with an assurance of peace, which no physical force or depraved teaching can disturb. Nor need this City of God fear any siege, regardless of duration. Fed with the full ears of the Eucharistic *wheat,* the Church has already withstood all that the powers of Satan can hurl against it, only to emerge stronger and more brimming with vitality than before. Proof enough is the dynamism of its present liturgical renewal after the long siege of the Protestant Revolt with its resulting subjectivism. And this has been achieved even amid the world-

wide onslaught of Communist propaganda and neo-
paganism.

> For he has strengthened the bars of your
>   gates,
>   he has blessed your children within you.
> He has granted peace in your borders;
>   with the best of wheat he fills you.

The historical Jerusalem, too, was once menaced
by overwhelming forces. But the Lord gave His people a divine guarantee of unfailing care for them by
pointing out His own faithful observance of nature's
laws. Through this psalm the same assurance is also
given men today, who see the Church in some regions
covered with the *frost* of mass apostasy, while in
other places the waters of sacramental graces are
frozen up by religious indifference. But the poem
proclaims that, despite this desolate winter of God's
seeming banishment, those same sure laws of Providence will some time usher in a second spring of
His redeeming love.

For instance, one may recall how the Father sent
His beloved Son into a world that had lain for centuries under the congealing cold of idolatry and sin.
But through His *Word* what a change took place!
At the breath of His Spirit the frost of pagan unbelief
melted away like snow in a tropical breeze, and the
sacramental waters flowed over the earth to make
it burst into a new and fruitful life in that baffling
phenomenon called Christianity.

> He sends forth his command to the earth;
>   swiftly runs his word!
> He spreads snow like wool;

frost he strews like ashes.
He scatters his hail like crumbs;
    before his cold the waters freeze.
He sends his word and melts them;
    he lets his breeze blow and the waters
        run.

Yet all this was accomplished by the same God who even now deigns to speak through His Church and who governs the world by laws and *ordinances* made known to those He has chosen as His spokesmen.

He has proclaimed his word to Jacob,
    his statutes and his ordinances to Israel.

Safe in this assurance of His continuous Providence today, every Christian can make this last verse a prayer for the conversion of those *other nations* who even yet have not been reached by messengers bringing the Glad Tidings.

He has not done thus for any other nation;
    his ordinances he has not made known
        to them.

Psalm 124—Man May Learn Wisdom From the Ancient Hills

Through all the wars of countless centuries Jerusalem, situated partly on Mount Sion amid the surrounding heights, has been practically impregnable. Christians too, so long as they remain within the Church, amid the enfolding hills of the sacramental graces, may feel just as safe from their own spiritual foes. This on one condition, however: placing all

their confidence in divine aid instead of in their own
self-sufficiency, they must resist with enduring
patience all the onslaughts of temptation.

> They who trust in the Lord are like Mount
> Sion,
>   which is immovable; which forever
>   stands.
> Mountains are round about Jerusalem;
>   so the Lord is round about his people,
>   both now and forever.

Despite all its natural defenses, Jerusalem was
nevertheless once taken and held in subjection by a
pagan power. This was because the Israelites had to
be punished for their unfaithfulness to the Lord.
Yet even in their subjection, amid the temptations
offered by the surrounding voluptuous culture, the
Jews were reassured that they need not succumb
even to the evil conditions they had brought upon
themselves. God would never allow them to be
tempted beyond their strength.

So also today. Fortified as they are by the ramparts of the faith, Christians too are living amid a
sensuous and largely pagan civilization. Therefore,
if at times they feel that they must capitulate to
some temptation, they may take a divine reassurance
from the next verses of this psalm.

> For the scepter of the wicked shall not re-
> main
>   upon the territory of the just
>   [a world objectively redeemed],
> Lest the just put forth
>   to wickedness their hands.

It is evident, then, that he who has been signed with Christ's cross is really committed to a lifelong war of attrition, which is likely to produce two kinds of human reaction. First, he does indeed possess the power, despite all the fierceness of temptation, to remain *upright of heart* and thus, by God's grace, prove himself as impregnable as *Mount Sion* today. For, although it has watched battling armies surge about it for thousands of years, it even now stands firm under the sniping of Arabs and Israelis still contending for its possession. So also one who is tempted may be sufficiently assured by such a symbol of spiritual resistance to emulate in his own way that same steadfastness.

> Do good, O Lord, to the good
> and to the upright of heart.

But how tempting is the other alternative in this long-drawn-out war of the spirit. How inviting and harmless-seeming the entrance to the many *crooked ways* of modern living! "Just a little lie" to smooth over an embarrassing situation; merely an assent of silence to a social injustice perpetrated by the "right people"; nothing more than a tolerant wink at a dishonest act one might have prevented. Yet for any such opportunism this psalm has a fearful warning: such ways are impossible to retrace without divine intervention. Regardless of how good the initial intentions, he who sets out on such a course will soon find himself "stepped in so far that . . . returning were as tedious as go o'er."[1] In such matters there is no middle way, since Christ Himself has already

---

[1] *Macbeth, Act III,* scene 4.

warned: "He who is not with me, is against me" (Luke 11:23). That is why the psalmist utters this dire warning:

> But such as turn aside to crooked ways
>   may the Lord lead away with the evil-
>   doers!

The psalm concludes, however, with a return to the Christian who resists even to the death. For him there will assuredly be protection and victory.

> Peace be upon Israel [the faithful soul]!

From the context of the entire psalm this is the peace, not of surrender but of bloody victory. It is the peace that even now in troubled Palestine broods over Sion hill, scarred as it is by the wars of history. For Sion's is the peace of an age-old wisdom that has learned amid the ravages of its ruins to see all things in their true perspective, that can view with equanimity in the long light of milleniums the un-availing efforts of all the warriors who once fought over its slopes, only to mingle their useless dust with its abiding memories. Long after all the tempests of men and of time have sunk to frustrated oblivion— even then will God's own peace illumine with its quiet calm that sacred mount, the symbol of His abiding presence among men. Such is the wisdom of that lofty height, where the fever of time meets the cooling caress of eternity and sinks to rest on the bosom of the everlasting God.

Psalm 61—No True Rest Save in God

Amid the constant and feverish unrest that marks this modern life the admonition to "relax" has everywhere become a byword. And who would deny that the mind, goaded by myriad plans and ambitions, is in dire need of some repose? The will, too, battered by conflicting desires and pulled this way and that by a variety of cross-purposes, begins to sag from utter exhaustion. By sheer force of circumstances, then, modern man may begin to live a futile kind of life without depth of thought or feelings. This means there is great danger that he may try to fill the vague hunger of his impoverished spirit with the husks of excitement and sensations; such illusions are abundantly proffered in a sort of drugged happiness based on leisure and wealth. Yet even so, there comes a time when the fantasies of fleeting pleasures suddenly crumble to dust and a person finds himself like a *shattered wall*, unable to stand without support. How many despairing souls in such a pass have sought refuge in drugs, alcohol, or even suicide. But on the other hand, many others, amid the wreck of their lives and even of their God-given faculties, have received the precious gift of a light from above, and this light has enabled them to enter once again into the creative depth of their Christian heritage to build their life anew.

Only in God can anyone find the rest which fills him with divine strength. *Only in God* shall he collect his scattered self and attain that vital, dynamic unity which makes him a person, instead of a mere agglomeration of emotions, impulses, and defenses. Only on the *rock* foundation of the divine will can any man today shore up his sagging purposes and begin to realize all the intrinsic potentialities of which he has never before dreamed. This is because the *rest* he finds in God is not a nirvana of quietude and inactivity but the fulness of all his powers brimming forth from Christ—the Source from whom all existence must start afresh.

The key to this creative depth is self-surrender. That is to say, man can build his life anew only by making his will one with God's. Only by immolating his life with all its ties and ambitions on the altar of the *rock* that is Christ, can a Christian draw thence the fruit of sacrifice in the wisdom, faith, and love that must henceforth be the dynamic motivating forces of his actions. This is why the psalmist ponders again and again, by repetition and refrain, the soul-shaking truth he has discovered; namely, that every human being is like a wandering and helpless sheep until it abandons itself into the arms of its Shepherd and Creator.

> Only in God is my soul at rest;
>   from him comes my salvation.
> He only is my rock and my salvation,
>   my stronghold; I shall not be disturbed
>   at all.
> How long will you set upon a man and all together
> beat him down
>   as though he were a sagging fence, a battered wall?
>   Truly from my place on high they plan to
>   dislodge me;
>   they delight in lies;
>   They bless with their mouths,
>   but inwardly they curse.
>
> Only in God be at rest, my soul,
>   for from him comes my hope.

He only is my rock and my salvation,
     my stronghold; I shall not be disturbed.
With God is my safety and my glory,
     he is the rock of my strength; my refuge is in
     God.
          Trust in him at all times, O my people!
          Pour out your hearts before him;
               God is our refuge!

The poet Francis Thompson once beautifully expressed the common experience of all who ever placed their hopes for happiness in such frail *breath* as *mortal men*: "I pleaded, outlaw-wise, /By many a hearted casement, curtained red, /Trellised with intertwining charities; /. . . But, if one little casement parted wide,/The gust of His approach would clash it to" by disillusionment or betrayal. For, unless weighted by Christ's own love for souls, any human heart will in a *balance prove lighter than a breath.*

Nor is physical force stronger than moral suasion. There always comes a turning point in human events when unbridled wealth and power have to match their strength with the Lord of history. So it has been from the time when His providence put an end to the mighty empires of the past. So it is even in this modern era wherein Christians may trust to find that, amid the ruthlessness of unchecked political and economic forces, *power* in the final reckoning still *belongs to God.*

Only a breath are mortal men;
     an illusion are men of rank;
In a balance they prove lighter,
     all together, than a breath.

Trust not in extortion; in plunder take no empty
    pride;
though wealth abound, set not your heart upon it.

A beautiful thought is the final one, which we
would do well to bear in mind all through the day.
It tells us that, despite man's seeming helplessness
in a world bent on attaining its ends even at the
possible cost of its own annihilation, there is still a
Ruler who holds in His hands more than the might
of empires. Yet this Omnipotent One, who rules the
destinies of peoples, whose decrees there is no ultimate withstanding, is at the same time said by the
inspired psalmist to possess the lovely, heart-warm-
ing attribute of *kindness*.

> One thing God said; these two things which
>   I heard:
>   that power belongs to God, and yours, O
>   Lord, is kindness;
>   and that you render to everyone accord-
>   ing to his deeds.

Psalm 22—Rich Pastures for the Good Shepherd's Flock

Even in Old Testament times, when people were
overwhelmed by the "law of fear," God was wont
to reveal His loving solicitude for a weak and erring
people under the tender figure of a shepherd.[1] And
Christ, who came to fulfill all ancient types, never
tired of reminding His listeners: "I am the good shepherd. The good shepherd lays down his life for his
sheep" (John 10:11). It is not surprising, then, that

---

[1] Pss. 73:1; 78:13; 94:7. Ezek. 34:11-16; Isa. 40:11; Jer. 31:10.

the early Church especially cherished this psalm, which set forth in figures easy to understand the wondrous mysteries that the Savior had accomplished for mankind. The first Christians clearly realized that they were indeed chosen sheep whom God had led into the fertile pastures of His Church, there to feed them with the divine life of His word and sacraments. This is why the "Good Shepherd Psalm" was one of the first taught to the catechumens, who during the Easter Vigil penetrated its deep significance while proceeding from their new birth at the baptismal font to their initial experience of the divine banquet, where the Host serves the servant with His own Flesh and Blood.

Since this psalm is so redolent of all the memories Christians ought to cherish, it is well for anyone now and then to ponder its verses so as to reevaluate the marvelous gifts described therein and thus cultivate a truly Christian attitude of mind. This would be a spirit of complete abandonment, without care or solicitude, to the Savior's loving guidance. For has He not said: ". . . my sheep are known to me and know me; just as I am known to my Father, and know him" (John 10:14-15)? Such knowledge on the divine part penetrates with infinite love to each one's innermost self —his many weaknesses, his undreamed of potentialities for good. In short, the Lord has even made the astonishing assertion that the bond of intimacy He has with His sheep is no other than the very union which makes Him one with the Father. With what utter confidence, then, can all Christians exclaim, *I shall not want.* For they know that they are continually receiving all the divine wealth of the Godhead welling from out the fullness of that Trinity of love and poured down upon mankind beyond human capacity to receive.

The Lord is my shepherd; I shall not want.

If, as the ancient Fathers agreed, the *verdant pastures* vital for the nourishment of the Lord's sheep are precisely the words of Sacred Scripture, one might easily conclude that the neglect of the Bible in modern times would account for the spiritual malnutrition and anaemia so noticeable today. No wonder many sheep are listless and myopic, when they lack the ever-fresh and invigorating food of God's own word to sustain them. This is the daily nourishment Christ would give His own amid the *repose* of contemplation—just a short pause for spiritual refreshment—before leading them out into the hazardous ways of their daily struggle.

In verdant pastures he gives me repose.

There is another momentous grace that Christians must never lose sight of, since it ought to have changed for them the whole pattern of their existence. This is what St. Paul had in mind when he told the Roman converts: "In our baptism, we have been buried with him, died like him, that so, just as Christ was raised up by his Father's power from the dead, we too might live and move in a new kind of existence. We have to be closely fitted into the pattern of his resurrection, as we have been into the pattern of his death" (Rom. 6:4-5). How was "our former nature [thus] crucified with him" (*ibid*. 6) except through the sacrament of baptism? Herein the soul, through a ritual imitation of Christ's death, is actually enabled to "walk in the dark valley" of His redeeming passion with the Savior at its side. This is because baptismal water has the divine power to produce in the soul the real and lasting effect of Christ's own death to sin and resurrection to a new and glorious life even now amid the shadows of this passing world. Such are the tremendous privileges of which the Good Shepherd reminds His own as they pray:

> Beside restful waters [of Christ's risen
>   power] he leads me;
>   he refreshes my soul [with new life of the
>   Spirit].
> He guides me in right paths
>   for his name's sake.
> Even though I walk in the dark valley
>   I fear no evil; for you are at my side
> With your rod and your staff
>   that give me courage.

Another characteristic of the ancient shepherd was that he often used his *staff* to guide the sheep, never to chastise them. St. Gregory of Nyssa further saw the staff in this psalm as a symbol of the Holy Spirit Himself, by whom Christ now guides and encourages the sheepfold of His Church on earth.

II

In the second part of this psalm, the poem changes its metaphor completely from that of Shepherd to the Divine Host who in the Holy Sacrifice prepares a banquet of His own flesh. It is easy to see why this psalm was the favorite Communion song of the ancient Church when she led her newly baptized children from the font of divine life direct to the table of the Lord. For He has indeed put to rout those *foes*—passions and temptations—which were buried in the waters of baptism and are now to be entombed under a new life built in the strength of the Eucharistic food. Christ has even anointed the *head with oil,* that chrism of confirmation, from which Christians derive their very name as members of the Lord's Anointed One. And so their *cup* indeed *overflows* with the sacramental joy of a "plenteous redemption" (Ps. 129) won by Him who said, "This is my blood which shall be shed for many unto the remission of sins."

> You spread the table before me
>   in the sight of my foes;
> You anoint my head with oil;
>   my cup overflows.

Those who meditate this psalm in thankfulness for all the marvelous graces of their sacramental way, may now turn their gaze into the future—to that revelation of the Good Shepherd shown to St. John in the Apocalypse. Here in the very court of heaven attained after a life ever sheltered by such goodness and kindness as only a divine solicitude could show, the faithful Christian may hope to find his place awaiting him among those who "stand before God's throne. . . . [And] the Lamb, who dwells where the throne is, will be their shepherd, leading them out to springs whose water is life" (Apoc. 7:15-17).

Only goodness and kindness follow me
all the days of my life;
And I shall dwell in the house of the Lord
for years to come.

Psalm 132—Living Together in Love

Behold how good it is, and how pleasant,
where brethren dwell as one!

In this beautiful psalm of Christian fraternity and
unity the Church Fathers have seen prophesied the
effects of confirmation. This is the sacrament which
crowns the initiation through baptism with a prodigal outpouring of the Holy Spirit, whose very essence
is love. Such ointment of fraternal charity, which
flows down even now over all the Church, inundating and transfiguring Christ's members, is nothing
less than the very Spirit of Jesus, promised by Him
as the seal of His undying solicitude until the world's
end.

To convey to the modern mind an inkling of the
deep spiritual reality that is Christian love, the psalm
offers a couple of exotic but vivid comparisons. First,
an all-pervading charity is like the anointing with
oil, which was poured over the head of the High
Priest Aaron, and which in its abundance trickled
gently down upon his beard, the symbol of his sacred
office as mediator between God and the people. Such
is the Spirit of brotherly love now poured out upon
the head of Christ, our own High Priest, until it
reaches His robe, which encompasses all the members of His Body today.

It is as when the precious ointment upon the head
  runs down over the beard, the beard of Aaron,
  till it runs down upon the collar of his robe.

That such a lofty ideal of Christian unity is still
possible, even in today's disintegrating world, the
poem goes on to assure us by this picture of abundant
grace ever flowing gently and fruitfully down from
heaven's height. The psalmist has in mind Hermon's
snow-capped mountain range, drenched with life-
giving waters, which in many streamlets bathe the
parched regions below, bringing life and fruitfulness
wherever they reach. Just so the fruits of Christian
unity and brotherhood will spring into abundance in
the Church wherever the Spirit is received with all
His refreshing grace ever poured out in Mass and
sacraments upon this arid world.

It is a dew like that of Hermon,
  which comes down upon the mountains of Sion
  [the Church].

As a Christian looks about upon society today—his
neighborhood, even his own family—if he fails to discern the signs of such Christian oneness, perhaps he
should do well to search his own innermost spirit for
some obstacle that dams up or turns aside those
abundant graces. Or, better still, he might reread St.
John's first Epistle, that document of love, in which
the apostle exhorts all who are Christ's:

  . . . let us shew our love by the true test of
    action, not by taking phrases on our lips.
    . . . When a man keeps his command-
    ments, it means that he is dwelling in

God, and God in him. This is our proof
that he is really dwelling in us, through
the gift of his Spirit (I John 3:18, 24).

Only on this condition can one hope for the fulfilment of the psalmist's last verse:

For there the Lord has promised his blessing,
life forever.

Psalm 14—Who Is Ready for the Sacrifice?

We of the modern world are liable to become so
legalistic in regard to our Sunday obligation as quite
to overlook the question of any subjective fitness to
co-offer the Sacrifice with Christ. How many times,
for instance, do most Catholics seriously consider the
condition laid down for all by the Savior Himself to
"be reconciled with thy brother first, and then . . .
offer thy gift" (Matt. 5:24)? Also our very familiarity with those awesome mysteries tends to increase
the lack of reverence from which our age is already
suffering. Therefore, as a preface to this psalm, it
might be well to consider the words with which Isaias
once sought to stir up the awe and respect of his people by asking this question: "Who shall survive . . .
the near presence of fires [surrounding the All Holy]
that burn unceasingly? . . . [For] those eyes [of
yours] shall look on the king in his royal beauty"
(Isa. 33:14, 17). Christians today, like the ancient
Jews entering into their temple for the mere figurative sacrifices, may find the answer to such a question in this short didactic psalm.

O Lord, who shall sojourn in your tent?
Who shall dwell on your holy mountain?

Before replying, let me examine myself first regarding the Christian ideal of outward conduct—moral and upright living:

He who walks blamelessly and does justice.

Then let me look into my innermost self. Do I always, in utter simplicity of soul, accept the good and true without distorting or seeking to compromise it?

Who thinks the truth in his heart.

Next, how about the social virtue of charity? Have I really taken as my practical norm of living St. Paul's canticle of love: "Charity is patient, is kind; . . . takes no pleasure in wrong-doing" (I Cor. 13:4, 6)? For even the ancient Israelite, to whom the theological virtues as such were unknown, had still this code of social justice:

. . . and slanders not with his tongue;
Who harms not his fellow man,
    nor takes up a reproach [he hears] against
    his neighbor.

How often even Catholics are tempted to pay lip service, merely for the sake of expediency, to persons undeserving of any honor? Or else, how prone Americans especially are to join in the cheers of the crowd for some celebrity, although they know that such adulation is lowering the general standard of values, both cultural and moral? But it sometimes takes superhuman courage to be one of those who do their own thinking in spite of social pressures, who honor the "egg-head" and the unsensational good man, while they show themselves unimpressed by the glamorized hero or heroine of easy morals and manners.

> By whom the reprobate is despised,
>   while he honors those who fear the Lord.

This brings me to the question: Have I kept the *pledged word* of those vows I made, when in the act of Sacrifice I offered my all with Christ, even though I knew it might cost me many material advantages?

> Who, though it be to his loss,
>   changes not his pledged word.

Has my total gift of self included, as it should, my material possessions? This would mean that, while I give for the love of Christ, I neither count the cost nor expect a commensurate return. The policy of "enlightened self-interest" is not found in the Christian code.

> Who lends not his money [for favors] at usury[1]
>   [i.e., demanding much in return].

The next verse strikes directly at the core of our present political life, where men's readiness to give or accept graft is the dry rot eating away the vitals of our democratic system. Yet the same tenet also applies to all individuals who must be on their guard

---

[1] "Usury against Israelites, but not usury against foreigners, was prohibited in the Law" (Boylan, *The Psalms,* vol. I, p. 48).

against influences that can buy their moral support away from right principles. For men may be bribed to favor a wrong cause or to ostracize an unfortunate person merely out of a desire to ingratiate themselves in influential circles. Therefore a genuine Christian today is one who

> accepts no bribe [of any kind] against the
>   innocent,
>   [regardless of his race, creed, or social
>   disabilities].

Having thus examined himself on the above practical Decalogue with compunction and sincere purpose of amendment, the Christian may now receive this assurance of God's blessing on any adversities he may encounter in his endeavor to carry out such a program in his life.

> He who does these things
>   shall never be disturbed [in his deep,
>   inner peace].

Psalm 129—From Depth of Sin to God's Redemption

Even in our baptized souls there is still much that needs redemption—much unfruitfulness, emptiness, and barren soil. But, whatever its form, Christians may use this void creatively by stripping themselves of all unrealities, meannesses, and self-will, in order to stand naked in the abyss of man's sinful insolvency before Him who is All-Holiness—but likewise infinite Mercy. This is just what one does when he prays Psalm 129, wherein the soul descends into the very *depths* of its need for redeeming grace. There, stripped of all pretense and excuse, it awaits in patience and hope the divine promises.

> Out of the depths I cry to you, O Lord;
>   Lord, hear my voice!
> Let your ears be attentive
>   to my voice in supplication.

If the all-holy God should keep our sins in remembrance, who of us could dare hope? But "what has revealed the love of God, where we are concerned, is that he has sent his only-begotten Son into the world, so that we might have life through him. That love resides, not in our shewing any love for God, but in his shewing love for us first, when he sent out his Son to be an atonement for our sins" (I John 4:9-11).

> If you, O Lord, mark iniquities,
>   Lord, who can stand?
> But with you is forgiveness,
>   that you may be revered.

> [Therefore] I trust in the Lord;
>   my soul trusts in his word
>   [i.e., in the divine promise of
>   forgiveness].

Anyone who has ever suffered from sleeplessness due to some great anxiety will know what it means wearily to count off the leaden hours while his soul yearns for the dawn. How much greater the uneasiness, however, if the darkness is a spiritual one, wherein the soul waits in near despair for any light of God's comforting forgiveness. Such a night may be due not only to mortal sin but also to some habit-

ual failing that a person has come to take for granted
as inseparable from his temperament. He may even
cherish it as intrinsic to his special personality. In
such cases God often abandons these souls to their
own devices, until they find themselves groping in
vain for the Reality they have lost. Then it is that
they must learn to wait in patience, like *sentinels,*
eagerly watching *for the dawn,* which will bring
back the light of God's reassuring presence.

It may be because some have not heretofore waited
thus, alert and eager for the least sign, that the Lord
has not yet been able to send the help they sorely
need. For He comes to our aid only when our dispositions are such that His grace will not be wasted
or rejected. If this should seem to require patience,
it should be remembered that patience is also a divine attribute, whereby God, untroubled in His own
eternity, can Himself wait in time through all men's
follies and uncertainties and indecisions, until they
come to Him with the full surrender of their free will.

> My soul waits for the Lord
>   more than sentinels wait for the dawn.

> More than sentinels wait for the dawn,
>   let Israel [my soul] wait for the Lord.

The psalm began with the soul's abasing itself to
the very depth of its sinfulness and need for mercy.
The same prayer ends on the beautiful note of that
plenteous redemption to which St. Paul alluded when
he wrote: "I give thanks to my God continually in
your name for that grace of God which has been bestowed upon you in Jesus Christ; that you have be-

come rich, through him, in every way. . . . And now there is no gift in which you are still lacking" (I Cor. 1:4-8).

Thus a person may know for sure that every supernatural good is his for the asking—provided only he remember that his holiness as a Christian must be altogether supernatural. It must be God's doing alone. Men themselves can avail nothing except in and through Christ. This is why the Lord often abandons them to the misery of their human weakness, so they may learn that "both the will to do it [work out your salvation] and the accomplishment of that will are something which God accomplishes in you, to carry out his loving purpose" (Phil. 2:13).

This is why the psalm would have a soul always end by throwing itself into the arms of omnipotent Mercy in acknowledging its utter helplessness when left to its own efforts. The bounteousness of divine grace is ever waiting until men make room for it by self-surrender.

> For with the Lord is kindness
>   and with him is plenteous redemption;
> And he will redeem Israel
>   from all their iniquities.

Psalm 31—The Joy of God's Forgiving Grace

This is one of the most consoling prayers in the whole Psalter, since it proclaims to all peoples and times that God's love is mightier than His justice; and therein lies the way of man's forgiveness. What is sin but the creature's repudiation of his debt of love to a God whose very being is the profound giving of Himself as life and love? Once the sinner has understood this, he immediately feels himself cut off from the very reason for his existence and consequently drifts into illusion and death. How can he ever return to a bond of love that he has severed by his own deliberate guilt? The psalmist answers that his *fault is taken away,* as if it had never been. Yet how can it be that the Lord of Truth *imputes not guilt* to one who has actually sinned? The inspired poet was able to answer this in his own heart by belief in the coming Redeemer, and so to anticipate the efficacy of His merits.

The psalmist, however, little dreamed—how few of the Old Covenant ever did?—that between man's state of sinfulness and his sinlessness must lie "a death, a destruction in which the sinner is submerged, in order to be lifted from it into a new existence."[1] Moreover, in this our era that same death and resurrection abide with wondrous fruitfulness in the sacrament of Penance. That is to say, every time this sacrament is received, although nothing of the visible circumstances remain, the Christian is actually plunged anew into the very substance of Christ's own death, so as to be permeated with His new-risen life. As St. Leo the Great said long ago, "That which was visible in our Redeemer [his death and resurrection] has now passed into the sacraments."[2] Cal-

---

[1] Guardini, *op. cit.,* p. 131.

[2] Louis Bouyer, *Liturgical Piety* (South Bend, Ind.: University of Notre Dame Press, 1955), p. 89.

vary itself was only one stage in the work of redemption, which was to go on through the centuries by means of the sacramental economy.

All those marvelous truths we of the modern world may read into the words of this psalm, which was inspired by an omniscient God as fitted for all times and circumstances.

> Happy is he whose fault is taken away,
>   whose sin is covered.
> Happy the man to whom the Lord imputes
>   not guilt,
>   in whose spirit there is no guile.

II

It was not left for Freud alone to discover the psychological benefits of confession. Even the ancient psalmist experienced the conflict between shame and conscience, as well as the much-to-be-desired peace of mind finally gained from his open acknowledgement of guilt. The inner struggle here described, however, lacks a modern ring, since to-day's sinner is more likely to seek refuge in some escape mechanism or condoning philosophy than to suffer such physical effects of a bad conscience as loss of weight, disturbed sleep, diminution of vigor resembling a premature old age—all due to the burning fever of his inner reproach.

> As long as I would not speak, my bones wasted
>   away
>   with my groaning all the day,

For day and night your hand was heavy
    upon me;
  my strength was dried up as by the heat of
    summer.

Suddenly all is changed! The soul resolves to confess the sin which, like a cancer, is eating into its
very vitals. Who is more competent to describe the
effect of all this than Augustine, who had lived for
years with his own sense of guilt? "The voice [of
confession] is not yet so much as upon the lips
when—the wound is healed!"[1] How like the instan-
taneous cures our Lord wrought in His earthly life:
"Lord, if it be thy will, thou hast power to make me
clean. Jesus held out his hand and touched him, and
said, It is my will; be thou made clean" (Matt. 8:2-3).

  Then I acknowledged my sin to you,
    my guilt I covered not.
  I said, "I confess my faults to the Lord,"
    and you took away the guilt of my sin.

After any experience of separation from God by
sin, the Christian can surely take to heart this advice
of the poet inspired by his own penitence. When the
flood waters of life threaten to engulf you in temptation, turn in faith and trust to God as an unfailing
shelter in distress. Here in the bonds of His love is
the only true *freedom* possible for a creature whose
sovereign will has long been made captive in the
slavery of concupiscence.

---

[1] C. C. Martindale, *Towards Loving the Psalms* (New York: Sheed &
Ward, 1940), p. 149.

For this shall every faithful man pray to you
　　in time of stress.
Though deep waters overflow,
　　they shall not reach him.
You are my shelter; from distress you will
　　　preserve me;
　　with glad cries of freedom you will ring
　　　me round.

III

Now God Himself speaks, showing Christians *the
way* they *should walk,* which is no other than to
follow Him in whose death and resurrection they
have just participated. This is why the grace proper
to the sacrament of Penance is described as a "con-
figuration to Christ,"[1] who by dying and rising to a
new life has become indeed the new Adam and can
therefore transfigure His members into His own likeness, "borrowing glory from that glory" (II Cor.
3:18). And what was "his likeness" during that
earthly sojourn, except a luminous example showing
the way of submission to God's guidance in every
detail of both the hidden and public life? Consequently, any Christian can now understand that one
who must be forced into submission to the Lord's
loving Providence only lowers himself to the level of
a brute, which submits to no other law but compulsion. On the other hand, the man of faith accepts the
bridle of divine guidance as the symbol of a Father's
solicitude ruling always for the best.

---

[1] M.M. Philipon, O.P., *The Sacraments in the Christian Life* (Westminster, Md.: The Newman Press, 1954), p. 209.

I will instruct you and show you the way you
   should walk;
I will counsel you, keeping my eye on you.
Be not senseless like horses or mules:
   with bit and bridle their temper must be curbed,
   else they will not come near you.

IV

The final strophe is an illustration of the social
spirit that should pervade all Christian prayer. First,
there is a solicitous warning for the thoughtless, so
that they may take heed and not have to learn this
practical lesson in the harsh school of experience:

Many are the sorrows of the wicked,
   but kindness surrounds him who trusts in the
      Lord.

Lastly, sin tends to hide in one's innermost soul
and there to devour the very vitals of his being; joy,
on the other hand, has an outward tendency to share
itself with others and to lift up all hearts in happiness
and exultation. This is why the psalmist, as well as
the modern Christian, after a backward glance of
compunction into the guilty past, now proclaims that
"life laughs with God's love again,"[1] a gladness made
possible only by love's death and the new creation
of risen life in Christ.

Be glad in the Lord and rejoice, you just;
   exult, all you upright of heart.

---

[1] Eugene O'Neill, *Days Without End.*

Psalm 130—Growth Towards Spiritual Maturity

As Christians move through the psalms in the spirit of faith and prayer, they may find that their souls, ever reaching out to new light and truth, are touched by a greater realization of God's unfathomable perfection. For if they consider the Omnipotence that has merely willed out of nothingness this marvelous creation, they cannot help being moved to deepest self-abasement at the contrast between that infinite Being and their own intrinsic nothingness. Thus they are filled with awe and reverence at the thought that this sovereign Deity should not only have regarded sinful creatures like themselves, but should even have raised them far beyond mere creaturehood to the dizzy height of sharing in His own life of immeasurable happiness. When they have thus reacted to God's self-revelation in the psalms, then there is born in them the true virtue of humility. This rock foundation of the spiritual life places a person in an attitude of deepest reverence, which means the surrendering of mind and will to God with the utter confidence of a little child.

Once so oriented in divine truth, the soul will soon begin to discover—strangely enough!—that the deepest things in life are found only by searching the abyss of its own nothingness. Thus it learns that to accomplish worthwhile things it has only to make itself so insignificant that God may be able to use it as His pliant instrument. The soul will see, above all, that any effectiveness on its part is directly proportionate to the abasement of self, especially of its own opinionatedness. For how could even Omnipotence

use as His implement one who is smugly satified with
the mere surface of reality? And so the Christian may
discover through this psalm that the only way to prepare himself for usefulness in Christ's cause is to bow
down his mind and will in profoundest self-surrender. Then God may shape that soul to His purpose by
filling it with His own light and love.

> O Lord, my heart is not proud
>   nor are my eyes haughty;
> I busy not myself with great things,
>   nor with things too sublime for me.

To make still more plain this difficult attitude of
soul the psalmist uses a homely but telling illustration. *A weaned child,* though treated with a harsh-
ness it cannot understand, reposes nevertheless *on
its mother's lap* with filial love and trust. The simile
implies yet more: the child by feeding now on more
solid food is ready at last to grow and develop toward
maturity.

> Nay rather, I have stilled and quieted
>   my soul like a weaned child.
> Like a weaned child on its mother's lap,
>   so is my soul within me.

This is indeed the way God deals with a soul when
it surrenders in real humility. He may require some
sacrifice of person or thing that seems to it as indis-
pensable as a mother's milk. Yet, if that soul still
throws itself into His arms with love and resignation,
it may rest assured that it has by divine grace taken
a momentous step toward its own spiritual maturity—
i.e. toward dimensions and perspectives in living

which constitute the privilege and burden of adult-
hood. Then depending no longer on the liquid nourishment of emotional satisfactions, but strengthened
by the solid food of the Holy Spirit, such a soul will
know how to curb any vain and self-seeking ambitions, as also to recognize and resist the puerile false
humility begotten of pride and human respect. Like
a child developing slowly but certainly to the full
realization of its powers, it will leave the initiative to
an all-wise Providence, waiting patiently but with a
full sense of purposefulness until it grows up "in
everything, into a due proportion with Christ, who
is our head" (Eph. 4:15).

> O Israel [my soul], hope in the Lord,
> both now and forever.

Psalm 126—The House of Christian Maturity

In the many wondrous deeds wrought by God on
behalf of His people there is always found a mysterious mingling of divine action with some requisite
human activity. For example, the Promised Land
was theirs as a free gift; but first with divine aid they
must exterminate its wicked inhabitants. Sometimes
even, as in Gideon's case, the Almighty would have
the leaders dismiss all but a token force, lest "the
Israelites would boast that they had no need of [him],
that their own strength had brought them deliverance" (Judg. 7:2). Or again, while He authorized
David's son Solomon to build Him a house of cedar
wood for the dwelling place of His Presence, He at
the same time promised that He Himself would build
David a "house" which would endure even to Christ,
the true temple of God (II Kgs. 7). Thus throughout

the history of the Chosen People the Lord showed an infinite condescension in allowing the intimacy of human collaboration with the divine work that was being accomplished. In this way He has ever manifested His desire to underwrite with invincible aid the efforts of man, so that, though remaining human activity, these efforts may be sustained and ultimately accomplished by the necessary divine intervention.

All this is very consoling in view of the task incumbent on every responsible human being; i.e., to *build the house* of his whole selfhood, with all its potentialities, into the mansion of his eternal abode. For whatever he makes of himself in this world determines what he will be for all eternity. This implies more than the acquisition of virtues, necessary and commendable as that may be. Every man coming into this world is given other raw materials for that *house*—his mental faculties and special talents to be developed to the fullest extent his circumstances permit, while the whole structure is to be shaped and modified to fit the unfolding of that personality which was the unique creation of an idea in the Eternal Mind. In short, each man must *labor* to develop his whole being—understanding and imagination, heart and emotions, will and feelings, even his bodily powers—until he reaches "perfect manhood, that maturity which is proportioned to the completed growth of Christ" (Eph. 4:13).

Yet there are many forces today that militate against the attaining of such maturity, the very concept of which is being much distorted. For there is too frequently an evasion of reality that produces perpetual juveniles bent only on a round of "fun."

How many broken marriages have been analyzed as due to "emotional immaturity"? How many beds in our psychiatric wards are filled by grown-up men and women who sought to evade their adult responsibilities in a childish dream world, from which they eventually could not escape? Too many Catholics, even, perpetuate their irresponsible religious childhood by resting in the smug satisfaction of possessing the truth, although they themselves make no effort to go beyond its periphery. Likewise, many so-called Christians seek refuge from the self-reproach of not growing up to their own ideal of self by assuming a cynicism that embitters their own as well as others' lives.

In consequence of all this, there is in the "free world" today a general and marked retardation of even intellectual development, despite the vast sums expended on education. This is doubtless due to the lack of spiritual foundations, which, by faith in the divine help and the urgence of a God-imposed necessity, would seize the initiative and motivate one's life for the required self-discipline. Even our phenomenal prosperity has removed from the ordinary way of home life the small responsibilities that used to train and mature a growing child. Therefore divinely fitting for the world today is the challenge offered by Psalm 126, which is an urgent summons for each and every Christian to realize the grave responsibility he cannot escape. And that is his need to build the *house* of his own unique person to the fullness of its maturity. For if Christians are in any sense unfinished in their own development, how can the Church, Christ's body, be "the completion of him who everywhere and in all things is complete" (Eph. 1:23)?

The psalm begins with the great paradox of Christian life, reiterating the often unrealized truth that any spiritual building must be done not by man's striving but by the power of God. Human efforts, though necessary, are nothing more than a response to the divine initiative.

> Unless the Lord build the house,
>   they labor in vain who build it.
> Unless the Lord guard the city,
>   in vain does the guard keep vigil.

In Ephesians 3:16-19, St. Paul gives a detailed description of just how this *house* of Christian maturity is built up. Writing in the formula of a prayer, he tells his beloved converts how important it is to lay the solid and unshakable groundwork of charity: "May your lives be rooted in love, founded on love." Then with faith to make a dwelling-place for Christ, the whole structure will be strengthened "through his spirit with a power that reaches your innermost being." Through that power alone will a Christian discover his true self and begin to become fully the person God's love had designed him to be. Next, when filled with all the plenitude God has to bestow, he will have attained a spiritual insight into his transcendent prototype. That is, he will "be enabled to measure, in all its breadth and length and height and depth, the love of Christ, to know what passes knowledge." Then at last a person may "be filled with all the completion God has to give." It is entirely God's work, this gradual taking possession of the Christian, who by surrendering his will is able to receive the divine grace proffered so gratuitously.

The next verse of this ancient psalm strikes directly at a very modern error, the heresy of activism; i.e., the conviction that action is of more "practical" value than prayer. These days the world is fast becoming absorbed in scientism, which looks only for facts that will produce brilliant accomplishments. In such a contest prayer comes off a poor second, since it produces only the intangibles of a deeper insight into the meaning of things and an ever-enriched inner life, neither of which can be weighed or measured in the laboratory. Such precious gifts are the fruits of the *sleep* of prayer, which stills the frenzied fever of activism, so that God may give *to his beloved,* instead of the *hard-earned bread* of high-pressured toil, a heavenly reward unattainable by human efforts alone.

> It is vain for you to rise early,
>   or put off your rest,
> You that eat hard-earned bread,
>   for he gives to his beloved in sleep.

God's *gift, the fruit of the womb* of prayer, is a numerous progeny of *sons*—i.e., valuable achievements surpassing one's fondest dreams. Conceived in the quiet of contemplation and nurtured to parturition by the Spirit of love, such acts go straight as arrows to their target, the greater glory of God. This accounts for the works of the men and women who molded history with only the weapons of prayer— Benedict, the builder of Christian Europe, Catherine who restored the papacy to Rome, Ignatius who

formed the forces that turned the tide of the Protestant Revolt, and Thérèse who from her Carmelite
obscurity shot her *arrows* over the mission field to
bring in as many souls, it is claimed, as Francis
Xavier.

> Behold, sons are a gift from the Lord;
>   the fruit of the womb is a reward.
> Like arrows in the hand of a warrior
>   are the sons of one's youth.

Happy indeed is *the man whose quiver is filled
with* such fruits of his prayer. As the ancient Israelite, facing his adversaries in the court of justice held
at the city gate, benefited from a strong bodyguard
of sturdy sons, so the Christian, supported by his
many good works done in the strength of prayer,
will have no fear when he, too, meets at the *gate* of
eternity the *enemies* bent on his lasting destruction.
For he well may trust that having sacrificed the human satisfaction found in worldly pursuits to give
himself to prayer, he has shown such abdication of
will as enabled the divine Workman to build and
fashion his soul and all his personal endowments to
"that maturity which is proportioned to the completed growth of Christ."

> Happy the man whose quiver is filled with them;
>   they shall not be put to shame when they
>   contend with enemies at the gate.

Psalm 110—The Christian Exodus

This psalm, originally the people's expression of
gratitude for their miraculous deliverance by means

of the Exodus, is equally apropos for the Christian today. That is, what the Almighty did for the Hebrews in historical reality is precisely what He is still doing for Christians in sacramental reality. The *works* are the same; only the form has changed. For instance, God personally intervened to free His people from Egyptian slavery; so also He still acts with the selfsame power and love to free souls from the bondage of Satan. Just as He led His people through the waters of the Red Sea, so also He still brings souls out of the blindness and illusion of original sin into a state of spiritual light through the signs of water and the words of baptism. Is it any wonder, then, that this ancient psalm has continued in use, that the Church has so treasured it as to make it one of her Vesper psalms for Sundays and feasts? Thus she would remind all never to lose their sense of wonder at God's works, which are no less marvelous in this era of sacramental action than in the far-off days when they were enacted in type for our instruction.

> I will give thanks to the Lord with all my heart
>   in the company and assembly of the just.
> Great are the works of the Lord,
>   exquisite in all their delights.
> Majesty and glory are in his work,
>   and his justice endures forever.

After the passage through the Red Sea the Lord brought His people into a desert, which was to be their proving ground before they should be permitted a triumphant entrance into the Promised Land. During that long sojourn of forty years how tenderly

He watched, while assuring them, through the luminous cloud, of His abiding presence. He even furnished them with miraculous food to sustain their lives. Yet this was but a dim figure of our desert sojourn in the proving ground of this earthly life. Here we too must be purified, trained and formed into a People of God, the Mystic Christ, so as to be fit for triumphant entry into the Promised Land of the beatific vision. And how solicitously God has provided for us also, giving His own guiding Spirit as our pillar of fire and His Church for the luminous cloud of His abiding Presence. Moreover, in what more *wondrous deeds* would mortal man ever participate than feeding on the miraculous manna of Christ's own life-giving flesh to sustain supernatural life? With all this in mind who could do otherwise than say with all sincerity these inspired verses?

> He has won renown for his wondrous deeds;
>   gracious and merciful is the Lord.
> He has given food to those who fear him.

Such interventions of supernatural power should, however, make Christians more than merely passive recipients of divine favors. For the manna, though wonderful, was but a faint foreshadowing of the stupendous mystery of the Eucharist. Food it is indeed; but it is also a dynamic force changing men so that they assume a new relationship, not only with their fellow Christians but even with all creation. That is to say, by entering upon this organic union of divine life with Christ, the New Adam, even modern man becomes instrumental in that great Design conceived from all eternity in the divine mind and executed at tremendous cost on Calvary—"to re-establish all things in Christ."

> He will forever be mindful of his covenant.
> He has made known to his people the power of
>   his works,
>   giving them the inheritance of the nations.
> The works of his hands are faithful and just;
>   sure are all his precepts,
> Reliable forever and ever,
>   wrought in truth and equity.
> He has sent deliverance to his people;
>   he has ratified his covenant forever;
>   holy and awesome is his name.

Such is God's eternal covenant, ". . . hidden from all the ages and generations of the past; [and] . . . revealed" to us (Col. 1:26). Before such infinite wisdom and everlasting love how could one do other than abase himself in deepest awe and reverence, which is what the psalmist means by *fear?*

> The fear of the Lord is the beginning of wisdom;
>   prudent are all who live by it.
> His praise endures forever.

SECOND STEP

THROUGH THE CROSS OF CHRIST TO ITS GLORIOUS CONSUMMATION

If through the preceding psalms Christians have poured out to God all their earthly cares, they will have found the vacuum of self-concern being filled by a new sense of oneness—even identification—with Christ. Then, as they continue these psalms, they will begin to realize more and more that it is Christ who prays in them. They will know that He has need of their minds and lips and hearts to utter and embrace the things today that complete the redemption in His Body, the Church.

Psalms 114 and 115—What Price Love and a Living Faith?

Most commentators are in agreement with the Hebrew text, which treats psalms 114 and 115 as one, owing to the internal evidence of their subject matter and structure. In keeping with this understanding, both the Roman and monastic breviaries have assigned the two psalms in sequence to the same weekday Vespers. Therefore, while numbering them

123

as in the Latin Psalter, we shall here treat them as
consecutive parts of one hymn of thanksgiving,
which formed part of the hallel used after the meal
at the paschal ceremony.

We know, then, that this very psalm was sung at
the Last Supper by the Savior Himself and His apostles. Matthew tells us that after the paschal meal,
wherein the Lord had faithfully followed the ancient
ritual, "they sang a hymn," the customary part of
the hallel (Matt. 26:30). Those words must have
come from the Savior's lips laden with all the meaning and cost of their fulfillment in the redeeming act
He was about to achieve for mankind. The apostles,
on the other hand, only much later realized that the
historical Exodus, whose memory they had just celebrated, was but a prophecy in type of the memorable
events they themselves were about to witness. For
the hour had now come when the true Lamb of
God was to be slain in sacrifice, so that His sacred
blood might save all peoples from the Angel of everlasting death, which held sway over a fallen world.
That same blood was to become a veritable Red Sea
through which all of Adam's race might pass in order
to reach, after astounding miracles in their desert
sojourn, the final enjoyment of the eternal Promised
Land.

Later on, in the full Pentecostal light, the same
apostles would ponder the truth that what Christ
had done objectively for men had also to be subjectively accepted by each individual soul in response to the initial gift of faith. This is what enables
everyone to enter with full consent of will into those
redeeming mysteries of Christ, prefigured in the Ex-

odus, realized on the cross, and made available to all men in the sacraments, the fruits of the passion. That is to say, every soul that would belong to Christ must indeed, by going out from the Egypt of its life of natural desires and satisfactions, pass through the Red Sea of His redeeming death. Then that soul must enter the desert of its own proving ground, where it will be nourished by the miraculous food of the Eucharist and all sacramental graces, while making its slow and painful pilgrimage to the Promised Land of its eternal destiny.

Accordingly, they who would undertake this spiritual exodus must know that the realities externally wrought by means of the liturgical rites must find fulfillment in their souls by integrating them into mysteries which involve their mind and heart and will. That is, the baptized should enter into the very depths of the Christian life—far beneath the shallow surface made placid by constant connivance and compromise. There must be a deliberately willed acceptance of all the circumstances which participation with Christ really involves: e.g., the sharing of His passion in terms of men's rejection, of distress, and a sorrow "even unto death." Any who have found the courage to go down with the Savior into that abyss, who have either surrendered all hope of human aid or have experienced its dismal inadequacy, who have uttered the cry of desperation to the One who alone can help, and have received their answer—such as these truly know at last what it is to *love the Lord*. That is, to love, not with the emotions, which are soon spent, but with a firm and undivided will, which knows no rival object.

I love the Lord because he has heard
  my voice in supplication,
Because he has inclined his ear to me
  the day I called.
The cords of death encompassed me;
  the snares of the nether world seized
    upon me;
  I fell into distress and sorrow,
And I called upon the name of the Lord,
  "O Lord, save my life!"

Once such a soul has entered resignedly into the deepest sorrow and there found Christ, it receives new insight into the mystery of suffering. This is a problem which tortures the mind so long as it seeks a natural solution. It achieves peace, however, as soon as the intellect recognizes that the weight of infinite love can be borne only by the deepest self-abandonment to the divine will. This is the lesson learned in the school of life where souls, *brought low* by humiliations, discover that merciful love is only for *the little ones.* Thus the Christian has his eyes opened at last not to human appraisal, but to a whole new scale of divine values with a *gracious* and *just* God as the center and starting point for everything.

Gracious is the Lord and just;
  yes, our God is merciful.
The Lord keeps the little ones;
  I was brought low, and he saved me.

"Only in God is my soul at rest" (Ps. 61:2). On this sea of infinite compassion the soul may recover its *tranquility* in the knowledge that Christ has transfigured sorrow and pain in the radiance of His risen glory.

> Return, O my soul, to your tranquility,
>   for the Lord has been good to you.
> For he has freed my soul from death,
>   my eyes from tears, my feet from stumbling.

The final outcome of such participation with Christ in His fulfillment of the Pasch is what St. Paul most desired that all his converts realize to the greatest extent. Recalling the wondrous things done to them by their passage through the Red Sea of Christ's death, the apostle tells them that there must be no going back to the Egypt of their old life. They are now dead, since their former life lies buried with Christ in God. "In our baptism, we have been buried with him, died like him, that so, just as Christ was raised up by his Father's power from the dead, we too might live and move in a new kind of existence. We have to be closely fitted into the pattern of his resurrection, as we have been into the pattern of his death, . . . the life he now lives is a life that looks towards God" (Rom. 6:4-11).

> I shall walk before the Lord
> in the lands of the living.

Psalm 115

Anyone who has ever seriously tried to conform his mode of life with a sincere religious belief has soon come to realize that faith is far more than an intellectual assent to a creed. It is fidelity to a Person,

whom he has discovered in the vale of sufferings as
the God of Love (Ps. 114). This Person now opens
up to him a whole new world, which he must seize
and on which he must build his life anew. As St. Paul
exclaimed after his discovering of Christ, "And all
this which once stood to my credit, I now write down
as loss, for the love of Christ . . . compared with the
high privilege of knowing Christ Jesus, my Lord; for
the love of him I have lost everything, treat everything else as refuse" (Phil. 3: 7-8). The apostle, however, like the psalmist, is here speaking not of mere
knowledge but of the wisdom that springs from intimate contact with Christ's transforming power.
And so the apostle goes on to point the way to what
the inspired psalmist has achieved—namely, the at-
tainment of a living faith through suffering: "Him I
would learn to know, and the virtue of his resurrection . . ." (*ibid.* 10-11).

> I believed, even when I said,
> "I am greatly afflicted."

Purified by pain lovingly embraced, and created
anew by contact with divinity, the soul now begins
to discern clear-cut distinctions never before suspected. In the resultant clarity it sees how often today vice masquerades as virtue, or else the two are
blurred into a meaningless jumble of subjectivism.
The world at large, having lost its fundamental respect for truth, has robbed things of their inherent
dignity and honor by besmirching the real sense of
words, even of the very meaning of existence, until
the Christian cannot but exclaim with the ancient
psalmist:

> I said in my alarm,
> "No man is dependable."

How can one living in the modern world protect himself from the fog of ambiguities closing in upon him? There is but one way in which the soul's clear vision can perpetually be renewed and in which the heart can be continually purified. Like the poet of old, the Christian must have recourse to that kind of adoration in which his soul, prostrate at the feet of the All-Holy, actually experiences in the depths of its being the Truth that is God.

The oldest form of such worship was that of a thank offering, in which the creature presented his sacrificial gift in grateful acknowledgment that all he was and had came to him from an all-bountiful Creator. The offerer, having placed his hands on the head of the victim to identify himself with it, slew it, pouring out its life-blood as if giving it back to its Maker. Then the worshiper filled *the cup of salvation* and, having lifted it up while calling on the Lord, poured out the wine over the altar. Such was the ancient thank-offering, the type and model of our Eucharistic sacrifice. Herein the offerer endeavors to identify himself, so far as possible in will and intent, with the divine Victim, Christ, while *the cup of salvation* has now become for all "the chalice of Christ's blood, of the new and everlasting covenant." Only now the officiating priest, instead of pouring out the precious contents over the altar, imbibes the chalice of salvation, which brings life to all the world.

> How shall I make a return to the Lord
> for all the good he has done for me?

The cup of salvation I will take up,
    and I will call upon the name of the Lord;
My vows to the Lord I will pay
    in the presence of all his people.

Having received a clearer vision of all reality from this act of adoration, the soul now perceives something of the divine values. That is, no matter how unimportant he may be in the eyes of the world, every individual is of inestimable worth in God's sight. Moreover, even one's death, though ordained as a punishment for sin, may become *precious in the eyes of the Lord* because it has enabled the soul, united to Christ dying as Victim on the cross, to bring forth abundant fruits of holiness. This is especially true of those who have so loved God that they would not deny Him even in the face of death. Of these the Church particularly sings in her Office:

Precious in the eyes of the Lord
    is the death of his faithful ones.

As for the "ordinary" Christian, who does not expect to rise to such heights of heroism as martyrdom—even he can claim a closer kinship with the Lord than that of servant. For every baptized person is truly the *son* of God's *handmaid*, the Church, since he was born of her to supernatural life at the baptismal font and nurtured by the sacraments in the Father's house. How many times also has the sacramental grace of divine forgiveness *loosed* his *bonds* and set his spirit free?

O Lord, I am your servant;
    I am your servant, the son of your handmaid;
    you have loosed my bonds.

Therefore, as she summons all her offspring to *offer the sacrifice of thanksgiving*, the Church rightly admonishes them with these words that have resounded down the ages: "Right indeed it is and just, proper, and for our welfare, that we should always and everywhere give thanks to thee, holy Lord, almighty Father, eternal God, through Christ our Lord . . ." To this all true Christians have been responding everywhere in word and act:

> To you will I offer sacrifice of thanksgiving,
>> and I will call upon the name of the Lord.
> My vows to the Lord I will pay
>> in the presence of all his people,
> In the courts of the house of the Lord,
>> in your midst, O Jerusalem.

Psalm 53—Did You Meet Christ with His Cross Today?

Christ's redeeming passion is far from finished. For God has devised a plan of coredemptive activity whereby the whole Mystical Body, now deified by the Savior's divine action, can play its part by making all its acts and sufferings those of the Head. This is how the many tribulations described in the psalms can be as true when read today as they were when the Lord fulfilled the prophecies long ago by experiencing them in His own physical body.

For instance, let a Christian look at the daily happenings of the world with a faith penetrating to the spiritual depths of things. There he will find Christ in the seeming helplessness of His passion wherever His members through racial discrimination are driven from a housing project or reduced to menial work far below the position to which their education and ability entitle them. Or again, one may discern the present passion of the Mystic Christ in hard-working labor unionists defrauded of their savings and afraid to protest their injustices for fear of worse reprisals. Wherever the helpless or poor are exploited and kept in subhuman conditions, there Christ may be going again to Calvary. So much of this precious suffering is wasted today because its victims do not know how to transmute it by their intentions into the pure gold of the Savior's redeeming work.

Christians, however, are one with all the sons of Adam by reason of their human nature; by this same humanity Christed in baptism, they can lift up all the poor and downtrodden ones into the embrace of the Redeemer, as they join all men to Christ in this His own prayer today:

> O God, by your name save me,
>   and by your might defend my cause.
> O God, hear my prayer;
>   hearken to the words of my mouth.
> For haughty men have risen up against me,
>   and fierce men seek my life;
>   they set not God before their eyes.

No sooner will a man have uttered that appeal for help than he may believe it already answered in some way, we know not how. For we may be sure that whenever Christ prays He is always heard. And the psalms are truly Christ's prayer.

> Behold, God is my helper;
>   the Lord sustains my life.

The prayer is next directed against the very circumstances that crush or persecute Christ's members: dishonesty, unjust laws, ingrained prejudices, and all kinds of social snobbery. Against these *foes* the psalm implores:

> Turn back the evil upon my foes;
>   in your faithfulness destroy them.

So far it may have seemed easy to be Christ's spokesman in prayer. But he who prays must now go a step further and *offer sacrifice.* The term here implies the living out of the self-oblation made in the Mass by first of all admitting that the whole life of all Christians ought to be sacrificial. How could it be otherwise when they carry back into their workaday world the living Victim's dynamic purpose to use His members as instruments in His present passion? Therefore all ought now to be fired by the supernatural courage of the immolated Savior and freely set their ways in His footprints, which are warm and aglow with redeeming love.

The individual Christian will probably find his own sacrificial life consisting of practical things to be done right in his own milieu. For example, he may see an occasion for braving the social pressures of his own group by befriending Christ in someone snubbed because of a physical defect, lower economic status, or an unattractive personality. Again, the Christian may have to uphold a moral principle like the standard of Christian modesty, when it is being derided as "old-fashioned" and "impractical" for modern conditions. Such actions could indeed make his whole day a sacrifice of praise, so that he may say the following verse with utmost sincerity:

> Freely will I offer you sacrifice;
> I will praise your name, O Lord,
> for its goodness.

Sometimes, however, discouraged by a sense of futility, such a man may feel inclined to ask himself, "Why should I lead this sacrificial life in the midst of a heedless world, which only esteems my life madness?" Thereupon comes the answer from St. Paul, who would have all Christians realize that they are insolvent debtors to Him who loved them and gave Himself for them (Gal. 2:20). That is, each soul can truly say in the conviction of its own redemptive grace gratuitously bestowed:

> Because from all distress you have rescued me
> and my eyes look down upon my enemies.

Psalm 3—Carrying Christ's Cross Today

There is an overwhelming burden of suffering in the world today: uprooted peoples, still homeless and unwanted, confined like criminals in concentration camps; millions of others dehumanized by enslavement; tens of millions, just emerging from primitive cultures, are helpless victims of disease and malnutrition. Meanwhile how many Christians, though giving generously to relief organizations, remain personally aloof from human miseries? How many even take refuge in the defense mechanism of indifference, so as to prevent the world's unbearable agony from really touching their own lives? In so acting, we have to a great extent lost a most precious quality of heart—

compassion—whereby, like the Good Samaritan, one truly suffers with those in pain or trouble. Such a virtue, though too often based on humanistic or sentimental reasons, can have its source in a realism that sees Christ Himself in each human sufferer. For the Lord established this truth beyond a doubt when He so identified Himself with any members of humanity as to say: ". . . when you did it to one of the least of my brethren here, you did it to me" (Matt. 25:40). This is why St. Paul was filled with such compassion that he could write from his prison cell even to strangers whom he had never seen: "I am glad of my sufferings on your behalf, as, in this mortal frame of mine, I help to pay off the debt which the afflictions of Christ still leave to be paid, for the sake of his body, the Church" (Col. 1:24).

Such compassion and suffering-with-Christ-in-His-members, is the keynote of this beautiful psalm, which puts upon the lips of him who prays an appeal for aid that actual sufferers may be unable to express because of their condition. But this prayer can be used today as the collective cry of Christ carrying His cross—a cross made well nigh unbearable by the accumulation of world guilt. This psalm, being His own inspired prayer, has the supernatural power even now to break the domination of evil on earth and free His members, at least in soul, from the overwhelming oppression of cruelty and godlessness now crushing them.

Many who cause such anguish in the present world may be directly bent on destroying the God they refuse to believe in; others are just criminally careless in their theory that might makes right wherever power prevails. In either case, they appear reasonably sure that there is no redress from any higher tribunal, that Christ's members on earth today are as helpless as He Himself was when taken prisoner on Olivet, while infinite Justice hid its face and raised no hand to save. Therefore, on behalf of the same Christ, now hidden in all mute and helpless sufferers, those who pray this psalm may voice for Him His own cry for aid:

> O Lord, how many are my adversaries!
> > Many rise up against me!
> Many are saying of me,
> > "There is no salvation for him in God."

We know that during the passion, while His enemies had their way with Him, the Savior felt nevertheless a shield of encompassing might which made His soul impregnable to the powers of evil. Filled as He was with the *glory* of a righteous cause, He could indeed *lift up* His *head* even amid the sadistic orgies of His persecutors. So also today, the same shield of God's protecting solicitude has saved many a victim of neglect or atrocities that would have crushed the human spirit, had it stood alone. The next verses, then, not only assert, but also help to obtain for every victim of man's inhumanity this firm conviction of Christian faith:

> But you, O Lord, are my shield;
> > my glory, you lift up my head!
> When I call out to the Lord,
> > he answers me from his holy mountain.

Whence comes this unquenchable spirit that defies every assault of hell? From Him who by dying conquered death and by rising to immortality has given His Mystical Body deathless life. This is what makes His members through all persecutions fearless and invincible. St. Paul asserts of every Christian soul joined to Christ, "You, by baptism, have been united with [the sleep of] his burial, united, too, with [the awakening of] his resurrection through your faith" (Col. 2:12).

> When I lie down in sleep,
>   I wake again, for the Lord sustains me.
> I fear not the myriads of people
>   arrayed against me on every side.

This sure victory, however, while objectively won by the Lord for His whole Body, has to be subjectively attained by each individual on the proving ground of his own time and circumstances. This explains the urgent necessity for all of Christ's members, wherever beset by temptation and danger, to send heavenwards the following battle cry for themselves and their needy brethren:

> Rise up, O Lord!
>   Save me, my God!
> For you strike all my enemies on the cheek;
>   the teeth of the wicked you break.
> Salvation is the Lord's!
>   Upon your people be your blessing!

Psalm 119—Trials May Be Transfigured

If, as has been said, all the psalms speak of Christ, contain Christ, this lament of an exile among an alien people must truly be the voice of God's own Son after He had come down into a sinful world—to be re-

jected. The whole psalm breathes an inexpressible
loneliness such as can be experienced only in the
midst of a hostile crowd. With what depths of truth,
then, this cry has resounded down the centuries as
Christ Himself, speaking through every friendless
soul, has in His agony appealed to the almighty
Father to save Him from the false and treacherous
accusations of His enemies.

> In my distress I called to the Lord,
>   and he answered me.
> O Lord, deliver me from lying lip,
>   from treacherous tongue.

Christ on the cross in the midst of falsehood and
treachery never even answered His accusers. But He
has given to His members, of far less spiritual stature,
this psalm to serve as an emotional outlet for their
resentment and natural desire of revenge. Otherwise
a weak human nature is liable to give way to self-pity,
until the wounds begin to fester and secrete the
deadly soul-poison of hatred or of a persecution com-
plex. This will not happen, however, if the soul in
trouble remembers how, although the lying accusations of His foes pierced the Savior's heart, He did
not defend Himself but patiently awaited God's justification, knowing that out of this darkness would
dawn the glorious light of the resurrection. With this
prayer on their lips Christ's members may be permeated with the supernatural strength of His own
silence and trust.

> What will he inflict on you, with more
>   besides,
> O treacherous tongue?

Sharp arrows of a warrior
  with fiery coals of brushwood.

When the Savior in His earthly life prayed this
psalm, He understood, of course, that the exile here
described was literally among the desert Bedouin
tribes, with their deep-seated antagonism to God's
people. The same verses, then, must have carried His
mind forward even to our modern era, where He
would see His present members praying with utter
reality the same lament. For they, too, being His
own, must necessarily feel themselves in the exile of
an unchristian environment with neighbors as un-
comprehending of their aims and ideals as were the
ancient Arabs. So the Christian today, feeling lonely
and friendless in his exile, may turn his thoughts
homeward in this psalm and through it offer up his
failures and frustrations, his natural cringing in face
of an organized and determined opposition. Then
all is made part of Christ's present passion, while the
sharing of it with Him not only lightens one's own
load but also His. It is thus mere mortal's wondrous
privilege to transfigure his own sufferings by making
them part of the infinite treasure of Christ's redeeming work, knowing that wherever such redemption
is operative, there the world's festering wounds are
even now being healed.

Woe is me that I sojourn in Mosoch,
  that I dwell amid the tents of Cedar!
All too long have I dwelt
  with those who hate peace.

Sometimes, unfortunately, this wondrous truth
tends to be forgotten in the midst of daily strife, when

a person's own sufferings may become so magnified as to shut out the perspective in which they should always be viewed. When such is the case, one can always remember with what devastating truth Jesus in His earthly life, as well as the Mystic Christ of history, could complain of men's thankless opposition to the things that are for their peace.

> When I speak of peace,
> they are ready for war.

Psalm 122—Life Is an Undivided Reality

Dating from the period in Israel's history when honor-craving Jews cringed under the scorn of their Persian rulers, this psalm is apropos today for Christians living in a secularist society. Such a world, indoctrinated in the spirit of self-reliance, is strongly inclined to be contemptuous of any individual who dares suggest by word or example that in this age of enlightenment man is not capable of living his own life without consulting any higher Power. This secularism has been quite successful in relegating God—if He is permitted to exist at all—to some far-off heaven where He is supposed to view with lofty indifference human problems and sufferings on this lowly planet. As a result the men of faith who dare to show conscious need for divine assistance are objects of mockery—or, at least, of polite disdain. Consequently many earnest Christians may find their own minds slipping into the groove of worldly conformity, and so they may be brought to regard business and religious matters as belonging to totally different and unrelated spheres.

By turning to this psalm, however, the Christian may orient himself to the reality of a far different world, one whose Creator is bent lovingly over it, while He either directs or at least permits everything that happens. To make this quite plain, the poem presents a word picture of an ancient Palestinian household where the head of the family, conscious of his grave responsibility, dispenses to each member, child and slave, according to his needs. Since everyone is totally dependent upon the father's generosity, they all await with intent gaze the slightest sign of his pity. It is the same with those today who believe in God's providence. Knowing His divine solicitude spent on the lilies of the field or even the sparrows, all who now cry "Abba, Father" (Gal. 4:6) look to Him in confidence that nothing can happen to them unless for their ultimate good.

> To you I lift up my eyes
>   who are enthroned in heaven.
> Behold, as the eyes of servants
>   are on the hands of their masters,
> As the eyes of a maid
>   are on the hands of her mistress,
> So are our eyes on the Lord, our God,
>   till he have pity on us.

But it requires great faith to discern God's providence in everything that happens. For there are seemingly natural events that can make a person feel like the helpless pawn of blind economic forces or—what is worse!—of some other person's ruthless ambitions or jealousy. Thus human beings so get in the way as to obscure the divine Hand steadily and surely

working out God's own designs. It may be that the
human agents who cross a man's purposes and wreck
his plans are deliberately intent on evil ends. Nevertheless, the Lord can write every individual life
straight even with the crooked lines of sinful human
machinations. Therefore the thing for a Christian to
do is look straight past the earthly element to the
divine. For, although these wintry storms of man-
made troubles now threaten to overwhelm his peace,
the spring of divine compassion is never far behind.

> Have pity on us, O Lord, have pity on us,
>   for we are more than sated with contempt;
> Our souls are more than sated
>   with the mockery of the arrogant,
>   with the contempt of the proud.

How very human is this divinely inspired prayer!
It shows that one may even complain outright to
the Lord and be sure of a sympathetic listener. Yet
—and this is from the supernatural element in the
psalms!—one will also find these verses bringing home
an important truth; namely, that suffering is as necessary in every Christian's life as it was in Christ's.

If the Savior achieved His redeeming act on Calvary as the object of derision and deadly hate, it is
only fitting that His members contribute their share
to the travail of redemption amid like circumstances.
So St. Paul thought, since he reminded the Romans:
"You know well enough that we who were taken up
into Christ by baptism have been taken up, all of us,
into his death" (Rom. 6:3). This means that the
Christ-life which Christians receive is given them so
that they may offer up their bodies, and all that be-

longs to them, as a living sacrifice in union with the divine Victim stretched out and crucified upon the world today.

And so it ought to be quite clear that God's inspired songs were never meant for spiritual Peter Pans. The psalms are really battle hymns and have so been used down the centuries by God's soldiers on all the fighting fronts of the world. Whether as hermits assailing the powers of darkness or as crusaders for human rights and dignity, all Christians have found strength to win the fight despite the contempt and mockery of their fellow men. This is because those who are truly Christ's never fail to view their life as an integral whole, with the spiritual and material elements welded into one great reality.

Psalm 141—The Christian Paradox of Sorrow and Joy

The world today is drenched with suffering and sorrow. Yet how much of it all is wasted! Or—even worse!—if allowed to seep into the innermost mind, it becomes a slow and deadly poison petrifying the soul in its hatred and resentment towards God. Of course, all of us find it only natural when in trouble to look for human consolation: to seek from fellowmen that kind of solace which acts like a narcotic whose withdrawal makes us very restless and ill at ease. Or else we may dwell upon our wrongs, real or imaginary, until we find ourselves enervated and empty of heart, without light and strength.

How different all that might be if we actually allowed the Psalter to form us spiritually. Psalm 141, for instance, would enable a Christian to penetrate beneath the surface of his all-too-ready human reactions, to go far down into the very depths of reality, there to learn how to shoulder his own cross from the Savior's example. Also from this psalm, which is truly the Lord's passion prayer, one may learn that complaining to God in the midst of anguish is not wrong, since even the Lord did this. While the murmuring of a mind and will in revolt separates from God, the humble plaint of a heart crushed by grief but with the will ever bowed in acceptance, is most pleasing to Him. Moreover, such is the solidarity of the Christian soul with Christ that all its sorrows, when accepted for love of Him, are actually taken up by Him, and so through Him cry unceasingly for mercy to the Father.

Even "our weakness assumed by Him then becomes a divine weakness, and it is stronger than all the strength of man."[1] But Christ conquered sin with its attendant evils of pain and death by remaining unshaken in the presence of diabolical temptation, using the cross as His decisive weapon. Therefore the Lord's passion is nothing else than the triumph of divine weakness over all the strength and wickedness of evil.

When the Savior came back to His bewildered disciples after the resurrection, He asked the momentous question that every member of Christ has had to face some time in life: "Was it not to be expected that the Christ should undergo these sufferings, and enter so into his glory" (Luke 24:26)? Thus we know that the innocent Savior, like a compassionate physician, reserved for Himself the dregs of the chalice of

---

[1] Columba Marmion, O.S.B., *Union With God,* (London: Sands and Company, 1934) chap. 3, sec. 2.

suffering and renunciation; while we have to drink only a few drops of the chalice. Why, then, should Christians not lift themselves up to that lofty height of faith which sees in every event God's will directing for the best? In union with the divine Victim, whose desire to share man's painful lot brought Him to death on the cross, the soul can share in Christ's self-offering through its own immolation, by accepting everything as if it came from the divine hands.

I

Having thus learned to see the Lord's sufferings not as something done for us, but as something in which we truly have a part, the soul may enter into the mystical passion today by praying the Savior's own words when His human nature shrank from the unbearable burden of pain and dereliction He foresaw. The fact that this plaint is *with a loud voice,* while suggesting the intensity of His prayer, also seems to anticipate its world-wide dimensions, when it should become the plea of the whole Mystic Christ on earth. With His heart bowed down in grief, our Lord poured out His lament before the One who knew His *path*; i.e., His whole career—that mighty leap from the heavenly throne down to His present plight: "There was a hush of silence all around, . . . when from thy heavenly throne, Lord, down leaped thy word omnipotent" (Wis. 18:14-15).

> With a loud voice I cry out to the Lord;
> with a loud voice I beseech the Lord.
> My complaint I pour out before him,
> before him I lay bare my distress.

When my spirit is faint within me,
you know my path.

II

Reassuring it is that the Savior knew, even in the midst of His passion, the many pitfalls laid in this modern world to *trap* the soul in its endeavors toward God. He actually experienced the frustration of seeking human comfort, only to find that the three apostles, unable to fathom the depths of His sorrow, had no word of consolation for His need. They could not even *pay* Him *heed*, so sunk were they in mortal weariness. Thus the abandoned Savior gives vent to the loneliest words in the whole Psalter, foreshadowing His utter derelection on the cross. After two thousand years of Christianity, that cry still rings out over the godless pursuit of mere busyness: "There is no one who cares for my life."

In the way along which I walk
they have laid a trap for me.
I look to the right to see,
but there is no one who pays me heed.
I have lost all means of escape;
there is no one who cares for my life.

III

Amid the wanton neglect of men, Christ speaks for His human members today. Appealing to the Almighty, man's only hope, He summons up the soul's absolute trust and self-renunciation, so that it may seek nothing of self, but only the divine will as its sure refuge.

I cry out to you, O Lord;
  I say, "You are my refuge,
  my portion in the land of the living."
Attend to my cry,
  for I am brought low indeed.
Rescue me from my persecutors,
  for they are too strong for me.

Now at length the soul is truly prepared to go forth from the *prison* of its constraint and misery, where, thinking only of self, it was shackled with gloom and anxiety. But having cast everything upon God in utter abandonment to His will, it is freed from that self-centeredness which held it captive. Having surrendered unconditionally in union with Christ dying on the cross, the soul is now caught up with Him in that bond of mutual giving which constitutes the "eternal sacrifice." For being one with Christ the Son, who receives all from the Father and gives Himself back to the Father, the soul's own capitulation to the divine will can now be consummated with Christ's in the flame of the Holy Spirit. Thus comes the realization that this is a sacrifice not of death but of life, not of barren suffering but of bountiful redemption.

That is how all *the just* who have entered with Christ into His sacrifice have learned to accept everything with thanks from the loving hands of the Father. Henceforth pain and sorrow, as something to be feared and rejected, have no more place in their lives. For with their renunciation of self it is Christ's own suffering that enters into them and, finding a place deep in their soul, establishes therein the Christian paradox whereby there dwell side by side supreme sorrow and uttermost joy. This means that through the grandeur of Christ's own surrender, a soul shares even here and now in His unfathomable pain—but at the same time in His immeasurable joy.

> Lead me forth from prison,
>   that I may give thanks to your name.
> The just shall gather around me
>   when you have been good to me.

Psalm 15—Final Participation in Christ's Mystery

According to some of their sermons recorded in the Acts of the Apostles,[1] both St. Peter and St. Paul leave no doubt that Psalm 15 was "composed by the Messias through the mouth of David,"[2] who probably never suspected the full import of his inspired words. For the Person who here speaks through the psalmist is completely immersed in God in a perfect union brought about by absolute surrender to the divine will. This is why the poem is permeated with joy, confidence, and a perfect peace possible to no one except to Him who is bathed already in the light of the beatific vision. Yet the members of Christ may also take these same words upon their own lips; but even as they apply to themselves these magnificent truths, they will realize how immeasurably far short they themselves fall of fulfilling the whole spirit here expressed. With these reservations in mind, then, the Christian today can make this psalm his

---

[1] Acts 2: 25-32; 13: 35-7.
[2] Patrick Boylan, *The Psalms* (Dublin: Gill and Son, 1949), p. 49.

song of thanksgiving for the great unmerited privilege of belonging to Him who "died for us all, so that being alive should no longer mean living with our own life, but with his life who died for us and has risen again; . . . it follows, in fact, that when a man becomes a new creature in Christ, his old life has disappeared; everything has become new about him" (II Cor. 5:15, 17). Nor need this newness ever wear off or become tarnished, since it may be renewed every day in sacrifice and sacraments.

Why, then, should not the modern soul feel something of the same compulsion as St. Paul, who prefaced the above words by this passionate assertion: "Christ's love is a compelling motive"? This should lead one to sell all the baubles of earthly life so that he can purchase "the best part of all, that which shall never be taken away"—not even by death (Luke 10:42).

> Keep me, O God, for in you I take refuge;
> I say to the Lord, "My Lord are you.
> Apart from you I have no good."

The same love for Christ should also make Christians see one another in a new and supernatural light. For as St. Paul wrote, "Henceforward, we do not think of anybody in a mere human fashion" (*op. cit.*, v. 16) because all are actually or potentially incorporated into Christ so as to be transformed into His likeness. Therefore one ought to say sincerely:

> How wonderfully has he made me cherish
> the holy ones who are in his land!

It is simple to love one's fellow members of the

Mystical Body theoretically and in the abstract, but it is not easy on the battlefield of temptation; especially is this the case if they stand in the way of the worship we pay to any of the petty gods in which our materialistic culture abounds. How many a Christian sooner or later comes to realize that in courting those *other gods* of vanity, ambition, or short-lived pleasures, he does but *multiply* his *sorrows*. This is particularly true of the broken peace at home and the subsequent sense of guilt, if our self-seeking ambition demands sacrifices to a god of success or social privilege. Therefore it is the part of worldly as well as divine prudence that the psalm expresses here when it suggests a peremptory end to such *libations,* with the resolve never again to revert in thought or conversation to deities that greedily demand more and more from their votary, until they have plunged him into the abyss of despair.

> They multiply their sorrows
>> who court other gods.
> Blood libations to them I will not pour out,
>> nor will I take their names upon my lips.

After a soul in its spiritual blindness has sacrificed all, its reward is nothing but raw remorse. Christ, on the other hand, has promised a hundred-fold of blessings to everyone who will heed the Bridegroom's plea: "Forget your people and your father's house" (Ps. 44:11). To illustrate that same abundant recompense, the psalmist uses an ancient word picture of a host pouring into the cup of each guest at table his appointed portion. Thus, he says, at the Lord's bountiful banquet each guest's brimming *cup* is nothing less than God Himself, the Author of all good. Moreover, it is He who holds it up by His sustaining power, lest human frailty let it slip and spill the contents.

> O Lord, my allotted portion and my cup,
>   you it is who hold fast my lot.

When the Promised Land was divided among the twelve tribes of Israel, the territory, marked off by *measuring lines,* was parceled out by lot. Naturally, some grants fell in more delightful places than others. In the Body of Christ, however, each individual's apportionment always falls *on pleasant sites.* For "God has given each one of them its own position in the body, as he would. . . . Thus God has established a harmony in the body, giving special honour to that which needed it most. . . . And you are Christ's body, organs of it depending upon each other" (I Cor. 12: 18, 14, 27). Truly can all these members here voice their gratitude for such a wondrous *inheritance.*

> For me the measuring lines have fallen on
>   pleasant sites;
>   fair to me indeed is my inheritance.

II

What each of us in today's "lonely crowd" needs most is the realization that we do not have to be an isolated individual, no matter what our circumstances. In fact, we are more likely to suffer from a sense of loneliness in the midst of a crowd than in solitude wherein God's presence is sought. That is, sought by a faith so vivid and alive that the soul cen-

ters all its desires and interests on Him as a Person
who knows more intimately and cares more pro-
foundly about that soul than any human friend. Such
a practice of cultivating the realization of God's nearness, difficult as it is in this frenzied world, would be
well worth while even for its temporal benefit; i.e.,
an inner tranquility not otherwise obtainable. For
who could worry inordinately over decisions, if he
had acquired a habit of turning to God in time of
crisis, instead of seeking vain solace in complaining
to his fellow men? Then one would realize the tremendous truth of that unfailing Presence and know
with certainty that He is *at my right hand*. Such a
living faith, however, is usually attained by a very
special grace as a reward for many years of striving.
To this end the following verses, if well pondered
and practiced, would help immeasurably.

> I bless the Lord who counsels me;
>> even in the night my heart exhorts me.
> I set the Lord ever before me;
>> with him at my right hand I shall not be
>> disturbed.

Thus fortified, the soul may now be offered another
cup, the one of which Christ spoke when He asked
His two apostles: "Have you strength to drink of the
cup I am to drink of"? Then He assured them, "You
shall indeed drink of my cup" (Matt. 20:22-23)—
but only after you are well prepared to comprehend
its meaning. And so the Christian today may read
this next verse as the words of Christ telling His
own now on earth what is still left for them to drink
from the cup of His death. For in the sacrament of

baptism they have already gone down into His mystical dying. He would have all realize that even physical death is only the consummation of our spiritual incorporation in Christ. That is, the Christian in dying but accepting the fullest membership in that saving mystery, the redemption. Therefore He who, speaking of His physical body, tells us in the Introit of Easter, "I have risen and am still with you," can say to the Father concerning His Mystical Body yet on earth:

> Therefore my heart is glad and my soul
>   rejoices,
>   my body, too, abides in confidence;
> Because you will not abandon my soul to
>   the nether world,
>   nor will you suffer your faithful one to
>   undergo corruption.

The Preface of the Requiem Mass, as if to overcome man's natural shrinking from death, thus consoles him: "The life of those who are faithful to thee, Lord, is but changed, not ended; and, when the earthly dwelling-place decays, an everlasting mansion is prepared for them in heaven."[1] The inspired psalmist adds that this blessed hope will be fulfilled by nothing less than the very vision of God Himself. Therefore the last verse tells of the soul's overwhelming joy when, having clasped the Savior's hand and descended with Him into the valley of death, it awakens to everlasting life bathed in the resplendent

---

[1] Cf. II Cor. 5:1-5.

glory found only in "the vision of [his] face, in the presence of which there is bliss for evermore."[2]

> You will show me the path to life,
>   fullness of joys in your presence,
>   the delights at your right hand forever.

Psalms 41 and 42—From Christian Anguish to Glory

I

Almost all commentators now agree that Psalms 41 and 42 were originally one poem, since they evidence the same spirit, circumstances, language, and refrain. Moreover, the first hymn would be quite incomplete without the second. Therefore the two, while retaining their numbers as in the Psalter, will here be treated consecutively, so that they may be meditated as one thought unit.

The two psalms together illustrate a great truth of the spiritual life; namely, that inner conflict can always become the occasion by which an all-wise Providence may lead the soul to greater heights— even to a vision of its eternal destiny. Moreover, it is a well-known fact that the soul's desperate longing for God, even in the desert of spiritual desolation, is the surest sign of its actually possessing him. An incident in the life of St. Anthony of Egypt illustrates this point clearly. Once after a severe temptation he asked, "Where were you, Lord?"; he received this answer: "I was within you all the time. For you could

---

[2] Charles J. Callan, O.P., and John A. McHugh, *The Psalms Explained* (New York: Wagner Publishing Company, 1929), p. 66.

not have sought me, had you not already possessed
me."

This exquisite hymn also runs the whole gamut of
Christian experiences inspired by an all-absorbing
desire for God amid the harsh realities of daily life.
Starting from the remembrance of the wondrous
graces which are our birthright, then progressing
through hope, humility, and complete self-surrender,
it finally attains to a glimpse in faith of the glorious
vision which is our eternal goal. Therefore, even as
the Christian of today prays this psalm, he will realize
how valid is its basic psychology. For the psalmist
reveals the conflict in any earnest mind whose starting point toward greater spiritual heights is necessarily a new and keener realization of its need for
the Source of all being and love.

> As the hind longs for the running waters,
>   so my soul longs for you, O God.
> Athirst is my soul for God, the living God.
>   When shall I go and behold the face of
>   God?
> My tears are my food day and night,
>   as they say to me day after day, "Where
>   is your God?"

How often amid spiritual desolation we hark back
to a sunnier past, to a carefree childhood when God
was as real as the sunlight or the air we breathed.
Does not the recollection of such bygone happiness
often have the effect of filling the heart with unaccus-
tomed tenderness? Thus it is prepared for grace by
sloughing off the hardness that too often forms, like
a callus, on the soul that has been worn by constant

friction against hostile surroundings. There is, however, still another remembrance that can greatly
benefit the soul at any time; especially is this so when
the heaven that once lay about us in the infancy of
our fresh baptismal faith, grows dark in the en-
croaching shadows of earth's more urgent realities.
Then it is most timely to recall how the newly baptized once mingled already with the elect in the communion of saints, while the boundaries between earth
and heaven were done away, so far as the inhabitants
of God's kingdom were concerned.

> Those times I recall,
>   now that I pour out my soul within me,
> When I went with the throng
>   and led them in procession to the house
>   of God,
> Amid loud cries of joy and thanksgiving,
>   with the multitude keeping festival.

Three times in the course of the two psalms the
poet uses an exceptionally effective refrain, wherein
a threefold repetition produces an ever-deepening
realization of his underlying sentiment, while the
poem builds up both thought and emotion to a climax. In the first refrain the soul, while turning from
the happy remembrance of the fullness of its baptismal faith to the contrasting stark reality of its present desolation, does not become introverted or discouraged. For the keynote is *hope in God* engendered
by a deep and abiding faith.

> Why are you so downcast, O my soul?
> Why do you sigh within me?

Hope in God! For I shall again be thanking
  him,
   in the presence of my savior and my God.

II

If the prodigal son had not been brought to destitu-
tion, he would never have remembered his father
and longed for home. Dostoevski, whose tortured soul
knew a desperate thirst for God, has said that in time
of misfortune man sees truth more clearly. Thus, too,
the psalmist would teach the modern Christian to
see the close and real relationship between spiritual
desolation and the soul's turning to Him who alone
can satisfy its hunger and thirst.

But the approach of one who is utter nothingness
to Him who is very Being, begins always at *Mount
Misar*, "the mountain of littleness," where the *deep*
of man's humility *calls unto* the *deep* of divine Mercy
even across the *cataracts* and flood waters of temptation and near despair. At such times all man can do,
from the twofold abyss of his sinfulness and creaturehood, is to acknowledge his weaknesses and absolute
need. Whereupon he suddenly finds himself no
longer engulfed in his own miseries but in the saving
abyss of Christ's own Gethsemane, which was a darkness before the dawn of the glorious resurrection. To
assure oneself that such a thought may be validly
derived from this verse, the reader need only refer
to the fact that Jonas, whom Christ Himself pointed
out as prefiguring His own death and rising again,
prayed this very verse while buried in the whale:
"Here in the depth of the sea's heart thou wouldst

cast me away, with the flood all about me, eddy of
thine, wave of thine, sweeping over me" (Jonas 2:4).

> Within me my soul is downcast;
>   so will I remember you
> From the land of the Jordan and of Hermon,
>   from Mount Misar.
> Deep calls unto deep
>   in the roar of your cataracts;
> All your breakers and your billows
>   pass over me.

Whoever meditates this psalm today may now too,
like Jonas, find increased confidence in the Lord's
aid. One even begins to appreciate some of the aspects of the faith hitherto unrealized or taken for
granted; for example, the unfailing availability of
divine grace and the marvelous gift of *his song*.
That is this divine prayer book, the Psalter, by which
the Holy Spirit forms anew in the words of man's
lips His almighty Word of perfect worship to the
living God.

> By day the Lord bestows his grace,
>   and at night I have his song,
>   a prayer to my living God.

But the soul's testing is by no means over. A man
may have vivid faith in the supernatural, may even
hope in God as the solid and unshakable *Rock* on
which to build his life—yet at the same time he may
be sunk in the depths of despondency, a prey to evil
forces that by their mockery crush his very *bones*.
Christ too in the garden suffered such anguish. Therefore in so praying, the Christian may unite himself to

that redeeming agony and remember that, even while bending under the storm of distress, he with Christ is still permitted to utter a very human complaint: "Take away this chalice from before me" (Mark 14:36).

> I sing to God, my Rock:
>   "Why do you forget me?
> Why must I go about in mourning,
>   with the enemy oppressing me?"
> It crushes my bones that my foes mock me,
>   as they say to me day after day, "Where
>   is your God?"

Again the refrain, but with growing confidence that it is no longer Christ's member who suffers alone, but Christ suffers in and with him. The Savior who was acquainted with all human sorrows—and rose again to victory—now prays on the lips of His least and suffering member this refrain of *hope* amid the world's Gethsemane today.

> Why are you so downcast, O my soul?
>   Why do you sigh within me?
> Hope in God! For I shall again be thanking
>   him,
>   in the presence of my savior and my God.

PSALM 42

III

"And now he was in an agony, and prayed still more earnestly; his sweat fell to the ground like thick drops of blood" (Luke 22:43-44). The Mystic Christ is still undergoing His redemptive agony today as He prays in His weak and struggling members for a power more than human to *fight* the good *fight against the faithless people* of unruly passions and against the *impious man* of a nature ever prone to evil.

> Do me justice, O God, and fight my fight
>   against a faithless people;
>   from the deceitful and impious man
>   rescue me.
> For you, O God, are my strength.
>   Why do you keep me so far away?
> Why must I go about in mourning,
>   with the enemy oppressing me?

Thereupon, just as the Savior in His agony "had sight of an angel from heaven, encouraging him" (Luke 22:43), so now in this psalm He prays in and for His members that the Father may send His ministering angels, *light* and *fidelity*, to console and guide all who are in need. With such aid from on high the soul, having watched with Christ in His agony, now is able to reach such a degree of self-surrender that its petition has become purely spiritual; that is, it asks for nothing else but a closer union with God in His *dwelling-place*.

> Send forth your light and your fidelity;
>   they shall lead me on
> And bring me to your holy mountain,
>   to your dwelling-place.

Thus is attained the climax of the two psalms, where the soul's dark night opens out into the dazzling splendor of eternity. By that complete surrender to God's will the soul has offered its sacrifice, which in the deepest sense means to enter into the very life of God, so far as this is possible here and now. Such a soul is indeed ready to *go up to the altar of God*.

What is that *altar* but a figure of Christ ever offering Himself to the Father in the sanctuary of heaven? There before the throne stands the great High Priest, forever "offering up the Victim that fulfills all things. . . And though his sacrifice was made in time, in the historical hour of his death, it is celebrated eternally, in the endless present. Ages pass . . . but Christ remains standing, holding his sacrifice before the divine Presence until the end of all time. . . In holy Mass this offering centered in eternity is constantly renewed [in a sacramental form], for it cannot be repeated."[1]

In that wondrous act the soul even now has a part. Making itself a *harp* of praise with every fiber of its being—its thoughts, feelings, actions, capacities vibrating with gladness and joy—it pours out its thank offering to the Lord of lords amid the countless choirs of heaven.

Thus the future victory of the Mystic Christ is seen as already made present by faith through the instrumentality of this inspired hymn. For in the psalms everything—the struggle and the triumph, man's sin and God's encompassing mercy—all flow together

---

[1] Guardini, *op. cit.*, pp. 465-466.

into the joyful victory even now open to every living person in Christ's mystery of the redemption.

> Then will I go in to the altar of God,
>   the God of my gladness and joy;
> Then will I give you thanks upon the harp,
>   O God, my God!

But such a thrilling sight is only to be glimpsed by the soul so long as it is still only a pilgrim on earth. For the half-scanned glory of that eternal scene is soon shrouded again by the mists of worldly realities, and the soul must return to all the grim features of life which before had made it so *downcast*. Yet things can never be quite the same, since the mountains of its earthly troubles, once measured in the perspective of eternal truth, must shrink to their proper proportions. Moreover, in the light of Christ's everlasting oblation the soul now sees that sacrifice is the chief ingredient in the life of all Christians on earth. For them, this consists above all in the patient, faithful endurance of whatever life has to offer. This is how Christ's members can follow their Savior and Head so as to help Him carry the terrible accumulation of guilt in the world today. Only thus can they break the power of evil; only in this way can they lift up their hearts to sing with unwavering faith the last two lines of this refrain:

> Why are you so downcast, O my soul?
>   Why do you sigh within me?
> Hope in God! For I shall again be thanking
>   him,
>   in the presence of my savior and my God.

Psalm 21—The Mystic Christ Must Be Crucified Today

This entire psalm has always been regarded by the Church as Christ's own passion hymn, since He Himself quoted the first verse from the cross; and so many details of His redemptive sufferings are here depicted that it is believed the psalmist must have actually seen the whole event in a vision. How else could he have described with such accuracy the piercing of the Savior's hands and feet, the casting of lots for His garments, His throat parched with thirst, and the boasting of the bestial mob as they wagged their heads and taunted Him to come down from the gibbet? They even unwittingly quoted verbatim these words from the psalm: "He relied on the Lord; let him deliver him" (cf.v. 9 and Matt. 27:43). All this was done, comments the evangelist, "that the scripture (of Psalm 21) might be fulfilled"[1] some one thousand years after it was first sung in prophecy.

Yet all that was not a mere historical event over and done with, as, for instance, the death of Caesar. Christ is just as truly being crucified today in His Mystical Body as He was once in His physical body. That is to say, He the Head, although now personally immune to earthly sufferings, renews in His members now on earth the mystery of His passion, so that He may impart to them its immeasurable efficacy. Therefore, since the Mystic Christ is still being nailed to the cross, the only way each member can belong to Him is to say in all truth with St. Paul: "With Christ I hang upon the cross" (Gal. 2:19).

---

[1] (Douay Version of Holy Bible, John 19:24.)

Christians can fulfill their part in this present-day passion of Christ by fully accepting their pains of body or mind and mingling these to indistinguishability with Christ's anguish as He hung upon the tree thrust into the hill of Golgotha. This means that, when Christians pray Psalm 21, they add to the chalice of His sufferings their own poor offering for the redeeming Sacrifice: the sense of abandonment they too sometimes feel when their prayers go apparently unanswered; their temptations to despair; their feelings of loneliness and of being misunderstood; even perhaps their self-commiseration, which turns a person in upon his own emptiness and causes a self-made desolation.

All such outpourings of self ought, as it were, to strip the soul of its garments; i.e., any human consolations with which it may have sought to cover its shortcomings, so that in the nakedness of utter self-surrender it may be ready to be nailed with Christ to the cross of His will and to accept beforehand all the consequences of this act. But we know, of course, that one does not accomplish this heroic act all at once. On the contrary, the laying aside of self demands a gradual, life-long striving until one descends with the redeeming Christ to the very nadir of existence—a realization of the utter negation into which all men have been plunged by sin. Only then, when bereft of every consolation human and divine, can each one truly say with the Savior his own *consummatum est*.

Therefore it is good to pray this psalm of Christ's own dereliction. For with Him as Guide and Support, the soul may actually live Christ's feelings in a mystical manner. Meanwhile, the Holy Spirit Himself, by means of these inspired words, labors to form within each one of us the reality of the suffering Savior.

A

It is a terrifying experience when, even in thought, a person really looks at Christ on the cross and comes face to face with the stark reality of God's justice. How dares mortal man then recall the injustice of his many idolatries in the self-centered, materialistic values of his everyday life? All such considerations ought to make the soul sink down, down to the very depths of its sinful nothingness, where it will find naught but utter loneliness and despair.

Only thus are Christians today made ready to pray with Christ the first strophe of Psalm 21, voicing in their person His desolation who "never knew sin, [but] God made him into sin for us" (II Cor. 5:21). Then, having plunged with Him into the depths of that sin-created abyss, they may through His own divine prayer be enabled to glimpse a ray of hope and confidence shining forth from the long history of God's merciful dealings with men.

> My God, my God, why have you forsaken
> me,
>   far from my prayer, from the words of my
>   cry?
> O my God, I cry out by day, and you answer
> not;
>   by night, and there is no relief for me.
> Yet you are enthroned in the holy place,
>   O Glory of Israel!

In you our fathers trusted;
   they trusted, and you delivered them.
To you they cried, and they escaped;
   in you they trusted, and they were not
     put to shame.

"All those who are resolved to live a holy life in Christ Jesus will meet with persecution" (II Tim. 3:12). Yet we know too that God has not only fitted the individual cross to each person's spiritual stature and strength but has also given him the power to remain on it even until death. Besides every one's particular cross of difficulties, which are due to his own personality, family complications, or economic status, the modern world has placed upon all its votaries the self-made cross of conformity; this is demanded by a society that has nothing but meaninglessness to offer—and quiet frustration. For the sincere Christian, living in such a world creates a terrific tension. He would like "to belong" by outwardly conforming to the *mores* of his "set," but his spiritual dynamics for purposeful living are liable to make him a stranger and enigma to his "friends."

Who has not felt himself in some degree the *scorn of men* when he refused to go along in the general pursuit of the great god Pleasure as the highest earthly good? What Christian sincerely endeavoring to promote Christ's teaching on love has not experienced the sensation of being dissolved *like water poured out,* amid the policy of "enlightened self-interest, which is accepted as "standard morality" in the world today? What member of Christ, endeavoring to work out in his own milieu Christ's design for happiness, has not found himself beset by economic and social arguments like a *pack of evil-doers closing in upon him*?

Truly all of us need this psalm today, this prayer of the Mystic Christ from the common cross set up by a world bent on seeking its own ends rather than God. Such a prayer engenders in the soul deep trust in the Sovereign Good who, having in all truth been our *guide* and *security,* will undoubtedly answer this present appeal to *be near* now in time of need. Even the Christian's sense of *loneliness* in the *grip* of all those hostile forces will be more than adequately offset by his conviction that he is truly being merged into Christ on the cross.

But this means that the Christian must accept his own crucifixion, never trying to loosen the nails so as to compromise "just a little" or strike back in self-defense at the *strong bulls* of hostility that encircle him. Only then may he learn there is no such thing as loneliness. For he too will find that, since with Christ he hangs upon the cross, "it is Christ that lives in" him (Gal. 2:19-20).

> But I am a worm, not a man;
>   the scorn of men, despised by the people.
> All who see me scoff at me;
>   they mock me with parted lips, they wag
>   their heads:
> "He relied on the Lord; let him deliver him,
>   let him rescue him, if he loves him."
> You have been my guide since I was first
>   formed,
>   my security at my mother's breast.

To you I was committed at birth,
    from my mother's womb you are my God.

Be not far from me, for I am in distress;
    be near, for I have no one to help me.
Many bullocks surround me;
    the strong bulls of Basan encircle me.
They open their mouths against me
    like ravening and roaring lions.

I am like water poured out;
    all my bones are racked.
My heart has become like wax
    melting away within my bosom.
My throat is dried up like baked clay,
    my tongue cleaves to my jaws;
        to the dust of death you have brought me
        down.

Indeed, many dogs surround me,
    a pack of evildoers closes in upon me;
They have pierced my hands and my feet;
    I can count all my bones.
They look on and gloat over me;
    they divide my garments among them,
    and for my vesture they cast lots.

But you, O Lord, be not far from me;
    O my help, hasten to aid me.
Rescue my soul from the sword,
    my loneliness from the grip of the dog.
Save me from the lion's mouth;
    from the horns of the wild bulls, my
    wretched life.

B

The Savior had first to undergo nakedness and abandonment; thereupon even from the cross He was given the happy vision of a new creation He was now bringing into existence. So also with His members today. They too must go down with Him into the blackness of Golgotha, where, amid their own soul's nakedness and dereliction, they will first discover what they never before realized—the pride and self-love which vitiate even the best-intentioned acts. Thereupon, if in the barrenness of self-discovery they give themselves totally to God's will with Christ in this psalm, then the Holy Spirit can remake them according to the pattern of that new creation which Christ won at so dear a cost. If they who are His resolutely stay upon their cross with the Savior, even their failures and frustrations may become creative; for these deficiencies are now wholly His. Thus may be found in this poem the gateway leading from the narrow modern world of concentration on self into the limitless horizons of the world Christ envisioned from the height of His cross as the glorious fruit of His redemptive suffering.

As the sacrificial holocaust of the cross draws to its consummation, it opens up for all who suffer with Christ the vista of prophecy; and they may perceive a time when all the ends of the earth shall remember the price He paid and will turn to the Lord in deepest gratitude. Now they will find that everything—even the slightest pain willingly accepted—possesses a new significance, having become rich in spiritual power for the furthering of that Kingdom. So they, made one with Him by fulfilling their sacrificial *vows* of

self-immolation, can see the tremendous trifles of
their little pains burst into a blaze of glory in the
flame of His spirit which now sweeps the earth on
the wings of their prayer. No wonder the Savior envisioned, as the powerhouse of all this new life now
kindling the world, the *vast assembly* of His mystical
members; He saw them replenishing their supernatural life in the redeeming Sacrifice, as they *eat
their fill* of His glorified flesh now become their food.

> I will proclaim your name to my brethren;
>> in the midst of the assembly I will praise
>>> you:
> "You who fear the Lord, praise him;
>> all you descendants of Jacob, give glory
>>> to him;
>> revere him, all you descendants of Israel!
> For he has not spurned nor disdained
>> the wretched man in his misery
> Nor did he turn away his face from him,
>> but when he cried out to him, he heard
>>> him."
> So by your gift will I utter praise in the vast
>> assembly;
>> I will fulfill my vows before those who
>>> fear him.
> The lowly shall eat their fill;
>> they who seek the Lord shall praise him:
> "May your hearts be ever merry!"

> All the ends of the earth
>> shall remember and turn to the Lord;
> All the families of the nations
>> shall bow down before him.

For dominion is the Lord's,
  and he rules the nations.
To him alone shall bow down
  all who sleep in the earth;
Before him shall bend
  all who go down into the dust.
And to him my soul shall live;
    my descendants shall serve him.
Let the coming generation be told of the
    Lord
  that they may proclaim to a people yet
  to be born
  the justice he has shown.

Christians then should find it inconceivable to waste any of their sufferings in purposelessness or attempted evasion. For their every cross is also Christ's; and as such it bears the fruit, never of futility, but of glorious accomplishment. Therefore members of Christ ought now to find it possible to reach such a degree of faith as to consider of small consequence the loss, if necessary, of all this world can offer. For in the end they will receive it back a hundred fold transformed by glory. They will also have a deeper realization that, by using Christ's own words from the cross, they are now His will and voice expressing not only His agony today but also His praise to the Father, while through His eyes they survey the marvelous fruits of His redeeming work. All this is for the true Christian the ultimate meaning of the cross. Through this psalm he will have come to know ever more fully how closely his own despoiling of self is linked to that beatific reconciliation for which the Savior died on Calvary.

Transition

Through all the foregoing psalms of the suffering Savior, Christians have been enabled to participate as members of the Mystical Body in the centuries-long passion. At last in Psalm 21 they have plunged with Christ far down into the terrifying void of His own abandonment by the Father. Having thus penetrated with Christ to the absolute nothingness of sin, they were enabled to discern, even in the darkness of that death, the first faint rays of the "new creation" emerging, when

> All the ends of the earth
> shall remember and turn to the Lord.
> (Ps. 21:28)

For through Him, to whom was given "the first birth out of death" (Col. 1:18), all "transitory creation is lifted into the eternal existence of God."[1] Even now the Father "has put everything under his dominion" (Eph. 1:22), saying

> "Sit at my right hand
> Till I make your enemies your footstool."
> (Ps. 109:1)

Since in the psalms everything flows together in overwhelming joy over the accomplished redemption, one who prays thus may already see the gates of eternity open and revealing the King who is established on His throne. Although His kingdom in its earthly realm is still amid the throes of battle, the believer may nevertheless discern already the final

---

[1] Guardini, *op. cit.*, p. 413.

vision of Christ in the glory He has won by His redeeming death. Now He has become forever King, Eternal High Priest, Conqueror, and finally the Royal Spouse of His now glorified Church.

Psalm 109—The King and High Priest Whom We Adore

The Church has shown great wisdom and psychological insight in making this the orientation psalm of Vespers on all Sundays and greater feasts. For she knows that the attitude of adoration required in the Office is not easy for us in the modern world. We must carefully cultivate it. Therefore, while we pay homage outwardly in performing the required ceremonies, we can through thoughtful prayer arrive at an inward posture of deep self-abasement before the One who alone is intrinsically worthy of adoration. This is because Psalm 109 presents to the mind a series of pictures, awe-inspiring, even terrifying, of a God who—though He may be petitioned in all our daily trivialities—is nevertheless the Omnipotent who dwells in majesty amid light inaccessible.

I

The first tableau places those who pray in the midst of the heavenly court, amid such dazzling oriental splendor that they would normally be overwhelmed. But they remember who this *Lord* is at the right hand of the Father. He is the self-same Christ who "was lifted up to heaven, . . . so that he might grant us fellowship in his Godhead."[1] And so

---

[1] Preface for the Ascension.

each time Christians recite this psalm they are privileged to share in the joy and triumph of that redemption whereby Christ, our Head, won His decisive victory over all the forces of evil and extended the scepter of His power throughout the world. Since today, however, breath-taking scientific achievements by the forces of godlessness sometimes tend to obscure the certainty of Christ's already-won sovereignty over human affairs, the opening verses of the psalm may be used as a battle cry of faith in a King who, no matter how much He seems eclipsed, remains enthroned in triumph.

> The Lord said to my Lord: "Sit at my right
>   hand,
>   till I make your enemies your footstool."
> The scepter of your power the Lord will
>   stretch forth from Sion:
> "Rule in the midst of your enemies."

That is to say, Christ rules despite foes who are even now bent on exterminating Him by hounding to death His members on earth.

Who is this invincible Warrior, whose Mystical Body is ever emerging phoenix-like from the ashes of ruthless persecution? For answer the psalm takes searching souls far back into the reaches of eternity. There in the Triune Godhead the Father thus addresses His Word, the radiant reflection of His own glory:

> "Yours is princely power in the day of your
>   birth in holy splendor;
>   before the daystar, like the dew, I have
>   begotten you."

II

If, however, God were thought of solely in the guise of a powerful monarch, man might despair of ever soliciting that celestial court with his uncourtly petitions. So now the picture changes. Here Christ is seen in His robes of eternal priesthood, standing always as Mediator between the Unapproachable Deity and a sin-laden Humanity.

> The Lord has sworn, and he will not repent:
> "You are a priest forever, according to the
> order of Melchisedec."

III

Again the scene changes—to a world-wide battle-field. Here omnipotent Love has unfettered his power for the conquest of men. The picture is not a pretty one. For there are numberless souls that will not surrender to grace until, after bloody resistance, all their armor of earthly consolation has been hacked away, leaving them utterly defenseless. Only then do they exclaim with a Francis Thompson, "Naked I wait Thy love's uplifted stroke."[1]

This is largely the world scene described in the newspapers—if we but read with the spiritual viewpoint furnished us in the psalm. Looked at from this angle, the modern world is indeed a scene of devastation strewn with the bodies of despairs and blighted hopes. But one who prays these verses can make them a means of expressing either his own surrender to Christ or else a fervent petition for His victory

---

[1] *The Hound of Heaven.*

over those who still resist the shattering conquest of
His love.

> The Lord is at your right hand;
>> he will crush kings on the day of his
>> wrath.
> He will do judgment on the nations, heap-
>> ing up corpses;
>> he will crush heads over the wide earth.

That such a prayer will truly bring results in spiritual reality is attested by the last verse. Here the
mystic Christ-on-earth, though wearied, humanly
speaking, from His centuries-long conflict, reveals
His source of invincible strength:

> From the brook [of his divinity] by the
>> wayside [of his earthly sojourn] he
>> will drink;
> therefore will he lift up his head [in
>> lasting victory].

Psalm 71—"Thy Kingdom Come"

I

Anyone who has ever been distressed at the lack
of real meaning in his too often mechanical repeti-
tions of the Our Father should be pleased with Psalm
71. For in it he will discover a new and deeper realization of all that is connoted by the simple words, "Thy
kingdom come." Here in symbols of earthly grandeur
is summed up all the ancient prophets had foretold
about the long-awaited Messianic kingdom. Here
also is painted in vivid colors the spiritual realm

which Christ actually established on earth, although it will not attain its full development until the end of time. Meanwhile the King, who has come not as a Warrior or a Conqueror but as a Judge, through this psalm still teaches the world what it could be like even now, if only it would acknowledge the principles of His justice. That is why this prayer is as timely today as it was three thousand years ago. When Christians here petition for the Creator-Ruler of earth to impart His own spirit of justice to the Son, they are asking that Christ's judgments for the common good may be accepted by temporal powers today, that His kingdom may come even now for the poor and weak and needy.

Psalm 71 may be considered, as it were, a connecting link between the Old and the New Testament, in so far as it literally epitomizes the Messianic prophecies; it also foreshadows the Savior's own teachings about His kingdom as told in the parables. These parables, so varied in subject matter, prove that Christ's rulership can by its intrinsic force transform all earthly existence. That is, ever since the momentous "hour" when the Son of Man established His reign by destroying the powers of sin, there has been in this world something operative and penetrating, which, though invisible, produces many visible effects. Although Christ told Pontius Pilate that His kingdom was not of this world, it has always been interwoven with human history, a powerful influence on the lives of its subjects. This is because in the kingdom of Christ His truth enlightens the mind and His love rules the will; as a result, wherever His holiness and majesty are acknowledged, men live in justice and peace. Such is the picture of the kingdom that the psalmist draws in the first strophe—not as something already realized but as something to be ardently requested. The element of prophecy gives assurance that an answer will come somehow, sometime.

Just what His kingdom would mean to the weak and helpless today, Christ has already shown by giving man a brief foretaste during His own short public life. Then the *poor* and *afflicted* flocked to Him as their champion. For the justice of His judgment rang out all over Judea, as He dared the unjust judges to prove their own innocence before stoning a woman they had taken in adultery. Well understood too were His imprecations on the rulers who "fasten up packs too heavy to be borne, and lay them on men's shoulders; they themselves will not stir a finger to lift them" (Matt. 23:4). How different is that kingdom as foreseen by the psalmist in his prayer-prophecy:

> O God, with your judgment endow the king,
>   and with your justice, the king's son;
> He shall govern your people with justice
>   and your afflicted ones with judgment.
> The mountains shall yield peace for the
>   people,
>   and the hills justice.
> He shall defend the afflicted among the
>   people,
>   save the children of the poor,
>   and crush the oppressor.

II

The ancient poet, even though a prophet, still had but the limited perspective of his own time when he prayed that the Messias-King might *endure as long as the sun.* How much more enlightened in long-range vision was the Seer of the Apocalypse, who could discern the glorious consummation of the kingdom, when the eternal Light would render useless all created light. For the Lord God, outlasting sun and moon, will be the radiance in which "the nations will live and move" (Apoc. 21:24). Such is the ultimate fulfillment of this prayer:

> May he endure as long as the sun,
>   and like the moon through all generations.

During the long centuries of the kingdom's "coming," however, Christ has assured us that His grace is at work. It is hidden away and unnoticed like a little leaven, according to the gospel; or, as the psalmist expresses the same idea, *like showers.* These rains water the earth and stir to new activity the wondrous life planted deep underneath the soil, until it becomes operative by bringing forth the flowers of justice and the fruits of peace.

> He shall be like rain coming down on the
>   meadow,
>   like showers watering the earth.
> Justice shall flower in his days,
>   and profound peace, till the moon be no
>   more.

III

Also the Lord once likened His kingdom to a tiny
mustard seed, too insignificant for general notice,
but with a tremendous capacity for expansion—if
only through prayer it were given its full scope. "Thy
kingdom come," then, is a petition that could be such
a power as would open mortal hearts and even conquer all opposing forces in the modern world. This
simple supplication could penetrate the enemy's
strongholds and right wrongs—from the sometimes
dubious decisions of our own law courts even to the
communes of China. For it must be remembered,
this psalm is prophetic.

> May he rule from sea to sea,
>   and from the River to the ends of the
>   earth.
> His foes shall bow before him,
>   and his enemies shall lick the dust.
> The kings of Tharsis and the Isles shall offer
>   gifts;
>   the kings of Arabia and Saba shall bring
>   tribute.
> All kings shall pay him homage,
>   all nations shall serve him.

IV

In this modern life the Christian's concern should
be for the actuation of a justice that will render un-
necessary what we now call "commendable works of
charity." For if the individual is recognized in all his
Christ-imparted dignity, living as he is with the

divine life won for him on the cross, then not only his *blood* or life but also his every human right will *be precious* in the sight of all. If modern men would but embrace the heritage of their Christian forebears and would find the kingdom where it now lies hid, then too even *his foes* would *bow before him* as the unsuspected goal of all their desires. So, with God truly reigning over their will and all their faculties, men would discover the eternal uniqueness of every human soul and would endeavor with all their strength to bring it to its destined place in the eternal kingdom which no other kingdom can ever fill. This would mean making Christ's standards of social justice and brotherly love prevail in the affairs of men, until the whole of modern existence would be transformed by His presence ruling and directing all.

> For he shall rescue the poor man when he
>   cries out,
>   and the afflicted when he has no one to
>   help him.
> He shall have pity for the lowly and the
>   poor;
>   the lives of the poor he shall save.
> From fraud and violence he shall redeem
>   them,
>   and precious shall their blood be in his
>   sight.

V

Should, however, one's faith falter before the tremendous possibility of making any headway against the brutal realities of this present world, the psalmist now reveals a hidden power always at work sustaining the kingdom and making it ever expand. Such a secret weapon is the continuous prayer of Christ's members on earth. The gifts they lay on the altar of their immolation are their precious sacrifices and sufferings which, placed in the chalice of His Sacrifice, are transmuted into pure *gold* of redemptive might. Thus His own members, through the unending liturgy that encircles the globe, even now participate in the life of the kingdom, when *day by day* there are innumerable souls that *bless him* in union with the Church through His own inspired psalmody.

> May he live to be given the gold of Arabia,
>   and to be prayed for continually;
>   day by day shall they bless him.

This is why the sacred poet, with his spirit under the influence of a power that transcends space and time, utters a prophecy of the kingdom which would transfigure the whole world of nature as a symbol of the spiritual realm. Seeing the Messianic age under the guise of a superabundant harvest, the psalmist foretells the plenitude of divine grace and the prodigality of its fruits in the form of good works reaching everywhere, from barren mountain top to teeming city. That such spiritual peace, the fruit of right order, may indeed clothe every hill and land like the foliage of spring is the petition of this verse:

> May there be an abundance of grain upon
>   the earth;
>   on the tops of the mountains the crops
>   shall rustle like Lebanon;

the city dwellers shall flourish like the
verdure of the fields.

Yet only with the consent of the human will can
the kingdom press forward; it can never force its
coming. Men must not only prepare themselves for
it and welcome its arrival; they must also strive for it
with eager longing. This is what the following verse
helps the soul to do as it opens wide its portals for
the King to enter and establish there His reign.

May his name be blessed forever;
as long as the sun his name shall remain.

That other hearts too may receive their Lord, this
paraphrase of "thy kingdom come" climaxes the desires of one who has at last realized all the tremendous
significance of that three-word petition, so often uttered by the lips while heart and mind were far
away.

In him shall all the tribes of the earth be
blessed;
all nations shall proclaim his happiness.

❊   ❊   ❊

The last two verses do not properly belong to the
psalm but were added as a doxology to end the Second Book of the Psalter (Psalms 41-71). They
possess, however, a peculiar appropriateness here,
expressing as they do a heartfelt desire that the
Messias-King may have an eternal reign because He
is *the Lord, the God of Israel*. Thus the modern reader
may see tied together the prophetic threads of the
Jewish people's long-cherished hope for an earthly

kingdom with the present partial realization of that
spiritual kingdom that Christ announced. For He
as Conqueror over death even now fills the whole
earth with His glorious risen life. Moreover, we of
the New Covenant know that when all mankind will
have passed through the pains bound up with any
transition from the present world to the glory of the
world to come—when man's assimilation to Christ's
cross and resurrection will have been accomplished—
then the kingdom will be set free and all its citizens
will live by the very life of God in a world finally
transfigured by His power and presence. The everlasting Kingdom will have come at last.

> Blessed be the Lord, the God of Israel,
>   who alone does wondrous deeds.
> And blessed forever be his glorious name;
>   may the whole earth be filled with his
>   glory.
> Amen. Amen.

Psalm 2—The Rider with the Two-edged Sword

I

Whoever prays this warlike hymn immediately
finds himself in an atmosphere of the vast and endless
struggle for domination between Anti-Christ and
Christ, between the Prince of this World and the
Lord of all the Universe. Of no other psalm does one
have so clear an interpretation. For the New Testament relates that Peter and John, forbidden by
Christ's own murderers to proclaim His resurrection,
had just solved for all time the age-old dilemma of

the Christian in the world: "Judge for yourselves whether it would be right for us, in the sight of God, to listen to your voice instead of God's" (Acts 4:19). Thereupon the whole congregation set itself to prayer "with one accord," as they recalled that this struggle in which they were caught between the temporal and spiritual powers had been foretold them one thousand years before by the "Ruler of all." He had said through the "Holy Spirit, by the lips of . . . David:

> Why do the nations rage
>   and the peoples utter folly?
> The kings of the earth rise up,
>   and the princes conspire together
>   against the Lord and against his anointed"
>   (Acts 4:24-26)

> "Let us break their fetters
>   and cast their bonds from us!"

That is to say, the psalmist, who in prophecy beheld the Messias as King and World-Conqueror, also had foreknowledge of how the nations and their rulers would act all down the ages. Always there would be rebellion against Christ; sometimes the whole world would rise in revolt with this cry of self-damnation: "We will not have this man for our king" (Luke 19:14). Although the anti-Christian forces cannot ultimately triumph, the psalm gives no assurance that they may not attain such local and temporary successes as may outlast the lifetime of any individual, whose faith will thereby be sorely tried.

For instance, one may not even be personally involved in the debacle of Christianity in Russia to be troubled at the strange ways of Omnipotence, apparently acquiescing in such constant defeat with the loss of so many immortal souls. Anyone tempted to feel that way, however, must soon realize that his viewpoint is still of this world, impatient to see results here and now. But the psalm would elevate the view of those who meditate its content, showing that Christ's kingdom is actually in the process of always unfolding and conquering wherever Christians make His interests their primary concern. For regardless of how enemy forces may surge around it and even apparently triumph, each living soul, with its invulnerable essence, is a kingdom that can be held for God, even though the body suffer death and annihilation for its witness to the faith.

II

Now the scene of this highly dramatic poem shifts from strife-torn earth to the serene ramparts of heaven, where the Omnipotent in the majestic repose of His eternity watches, first in derision then in anger, men's futile efforts to "be like gods" (Gen. 3:5). Then at last the Lord intervenes to proclaim His divine Son's universal kingship:

> He who is throned in heaven laughs;
>   the Lord derides them.
> Then in anger he speaks to them;
>   he terrifies them in his wrath:
> "I myself have set up my king
>   on Sion, my holy mountain."

Here one could well pause to consider prophecy and fulfilment—as it were, two sides of a coin. For the same Deity who could terrify *in his wrath* through the words of the prophet, has in our time spoken to us through His own Son who, as "the full expression of his being" (Heb. 1:3) told us this: "God so loved the world, that he gave up his only-begotten Son, that those who believe in him may not perish, but have eternal life. When God sent his Son into the world, it was not to reject the world, but so that the world might find salvation through him" (John 3:16-17).

III

Again the inspired Acts of the Apostles offers the key for interpreting the next verse: ". . . there was a promise made to our forefathers, and this promise God has redeemed for our posterity, by raising Jesus to life. Thus it is written in the second Psalm, Thou art my son; I have begotten thee this day" (Acts 13:33). So did the Father bear witness to His Son through the resurrection, as He had also attested His own divine paternity in almost identical words when, after the baptism, He Himself had spoken from the cloud: "Thou art my beloved Son" (Luke 3:22; Mark 1:11). Moreover, as if to strengthen men's faith to the uttermost, Christ also has asserted His divine sonship in the face of certain death, while *the peoples uttered folly* and *the princes conspired together* for His condemnation: "You will see the Son of Man again, when he is seated at the right hand of power" (Matt. 26:64).

> I will proclaim the decree of the Lord:
> The Lord said to me, "You are my son;
> this [eternal] day I have begotten you.
> Ask of me and I will give you
> the nations for an inheritance
> and the ends of the earth for your
> possession."

In the Apocalypse, St. John has described the vision of what is actually taking place today in the invisible realm of the spiritual. He depicts this Son as the rider on a white horse, who wins all wars with the two-edged sword coming from His mouth; for He is the eternally speaking Word uttered first in heaven by the Father, now on earth through those who teach His truth. He also rules the world *with an iron rod* because He is absolute master of all events, and nothing can happen without His permissive will (Apoc. 19:11-16). That same *rod* has already crushed many world empires, making room for the triumphant progress of His Church, which is miraculously preserved even from enemies within. Although they have torn her asunder, they could never destroy her immortal risen life.

> "You shall rule them with an iron rod;
> you shall shatter them like an earthen
> dish."

IV

Today the last strophe is addressed to all Christians, who are truly *kings*, since they must ever rule over themselves and keep their passions under proper governance. All such should take warning from this prophetic psalm, so as to *serve the Lord* with becoming reverence for His holiness, even while they *rejoice* over all the assurances of eventual triumph given them in the wondrous prophecies that have been fulfilled.

> And now, O kings, give heed;
> take warning, you rulers of the earth.
> Serve the Lord with fear, and rejoice before
> him.

Rich as it is already in prophetic lore, the psalm ends with one more prophecy yet to be realized—i.e., Christ's second coming. Then, after all existence has been flooded with infinite truth and light, those enemies, once so bold, will shrink into themselves while calling on the very mountains to cover them. For everything that once helped them to conceal their hidden rottenness will be burned away by that righteous wrath. Then will they learn that He who "treads out for them the wine press, whose wine is the avenging anger of almighty God," bears this title written on His cloak for all to see: "The King of kings, and the Lord of lords" (Apoc. 19:15-16).

> With trembling pay homage to him,
> Lest he be angry and you perish from the
> way,
> when his anger blazes suddenly.

But all those who amid earth's mists and rugged ways acknowledged His sovereign power and sought, despite all obstacles, to make His design their paramount concern—such as these will now have abound-

ing joy in finding themselves united forever to the
very Source of eternal life.

Happy are all who take refuge in him!

Psalm 111—Christ in Glory, Man's Pledge of Victory

Although this is usually classified as a didactic
psalm, the Church's choice of it for Vespers on the
"Lord's Day" indicates that the *man* she has in mind
could be the Savior Himself. This is all the more
evident when we recall that Christ was so submissive
to the Father's *commands* that He even "accepted an
obedience which brought him to death, death on a
cross" (Phil. 2:8). Therefore the Lord Jesus Christ
now dwells in the glory of God the Father, enjoying
not only His beatitude as Eternal Word but also the
well-earned happiness of one who as man has won
the prize of blessedness. He did this, moreover, because out of *fear*—i.e., reverence for the Father's will
—He had chosen the cross and "made light of its
shame" (Heb. 12:2).

Happy the man who fears the Lord,
who greatly delights in his commands.

In thus redeeming mankind by His death Christ
did more than pay its debt of sin; He gave the human
race a new beginning. As a Second Adam He has
made possible a new and supernatural life for all
who come under His headship through faith and
baptism. For two thousand years this new *posterity,*
born from the pierced side of the Crucified, has
proved itself *mighty* against all opposing powers by
reason of Christ's own decisive victory over sin and

death. How else explain its thriving through centuries of persecution? How else account for its emerging today in the lustihood of new vigor from the catacombs of four hundred years of determined contempt and vilification? In such phenomena there is no other meaning than this: so long as Christians remain *upright*, fearing the Lord, they will be *blessed* with a strength far beyond mortal endowment.

> His posterity shall be mighty upon the
>   earth;
>   the upright generation shall be blessed.

That Christ's progeny should ever have fallen upon evil days is thus utterly inexcusable. For the Savior had endowed His own with inexhaustible *wealth* in the sacraments, which can fill reborn souls with all the riches of divine power made theirs for the asking. Besides, He is Himself the *light* that shows Christians the way through all the mists and shadows of earth, provided they are *upright* enough to follow His guidance, instead of trying to grope through the darkness in the pride of their own self-sufficiency.

> Wealth and riches shall be in his house;
>   his generosity shall endure forever.
> He dawns through the darkness, a light for
>   the upright;
>   he is gracious and merciful and just.

How *gracious* and *just* indeed is Christ, who always *lends* His talents of grace and opportunity, so that all men receive in accordance with their individual ability to repay. Even more: the Lord has also left to His Church a means of transmuting into the gold of eternal values the lowliest talent received. For in the Mass, whereby He is kept *in everlasting remembrance* on earth, all may place the earnings of their niggardly service, and Christ graciously makes these part of His all-atoning Sacrifice. Moreover, He actually deigns to need those paltry pennies, since He offers His Sacrifice now not merely in His physical body of Calvary but also in His Mystical Body on earth today.

> Well for the man who is gracious and lends,
>   who conducts his affairs with justice;
> He shall never be moved;
>   the just man shall be in everlasting re-
>   membrance.

Having in His mortal body conquered sin and death, now even in His Mystical Body on earth Christ has no cause to fear any evil force of men or demons. That is to say, the Christian also, being "deified" in baptism by the victorious risen Christ, must come to realize that, regardless of what any earthly powers may do to his physical being, they can never harm his soul, which is actually alive even now with the seed of divine immortality. Therefore, no matter what evil report a person may have to endure, he with the Christ living within him can hope to stand firm. There is no possible need to fear while one remembers that he is truly a part of Him who has already won the decisive victory—that anyone who stands with the Head can in Him *look down upon his foes.*

An evil report he shall not fear;
    his heart is firm, trusting in the Lord.
His heart is steadfast; he shall not fear
    till he looks down upon his foes.

Has anyone ever given so bountifully *to the poor* [unredeemed humanity] as the Savior, who, though "his nature is from the first divine, . . . dispossessed himself and took the nature of a slave" (Phil. 2:6-7)? Such generosity has borne immortal fruit, not only in souls redeemed but also in the glory that He receives. For "everything in heaven and on earth and under the earth must bend the knee before that name of Jesus . . . dwelling in the glory of God the Father" (Phil 2:10-11).

Lavishly he gives to the poor;
    his generosity shall endure forever;
    his horn [of power] shall be exalted in
        glory.

Henceforth immune to earthly trials and sufferings, the reigning Christ teaches all that they too must dispossess themselves of everything that is not His. Having thus renounced the false master of temporal things, *the wicked man,* Christians may come to face squarely the problem of evil and accept the life-long conflict that it lays upon every son of Adam. The members of Christ's body on earth can do this with the utmost confidence. For they are rendered invincible by the boundless efficacy of the Savior's triumphant passion communicated to all His followers. By means of their own voluntary death-to-the-world in and with the gloriously reigning Lord,

they too may render all the devil's attacks so in-
effectual that

> The wicked man shall see it and be vexed;
> he shall gnash his teeth and pine away;
> the desire of the wicked shall perish.

Psalm 44—Nuptial Song for Christ and His Church

The unfathomable mystery of God's love for man
has been expressed in many ways in Old Testament
lore. But no figure is half so appealing as that of a
marriage, wherein the divine Bridegroom seeks out
the love and faithfulness of lowly humanity to make
her His Bride. While many prophets in their teachings developed this theme, Osee beautifully exem-
plified it even in his life by a loving faithfulness to
the wanton woman whom God had commanded him
to wed. Nowhere, however, is the figure of this di-
vine-human espousal more exquisitely set forth than
in Psalm 44, to which Catholic commentators—and
even Jewish teachers—have given not a literal but a
mystical interpretation. Therefore one need not hesi-
tate to pray this psalm with the understanding that
the Bridegroom is none other than the Messiah-King,
Christ Himself, while the Bride represents the
Church of the Old Testament period, who has been
painstakingly brought to maturity and perfection,
so that she may be joined at long last to her divine
Spouse in the mystic marriage of the New Dispensation. And so now, in this era of redemption, as St.
Paul explains in speaking of marriage, "The man is
the head to which the woman's body is united, just

as Christ is the head of the Church, he, the Saviour on whom the safety of his body depends. . . . Yes, those words are a high mystery, and I am applying them here to Christ and his Church" (Eph. 5:23, 32).

It would be well to pause a moment and consider why infinite Wisdom should have bequeathed to His creatures so sublime a mystery expressed in one short poem—a poem that ought to be pondered not once but frequently. One reason is that the psalms, being inspired, possess in themselves a divine dynamism whereby the deep significance of their truths can be progressively realized by an ever more penetrating insight on the part of one who uses them assiduously. Besides, each time this psalm of the mystic espousal is prayed with true devotion the union between Christ and the Church—between Christ and that soul—is strengthened and vitalized by all the power of the divine reality therein contained.

I

If we consider how sublime is the psalmist's theme and how humanly appealing, we are not surprised that the inspired poet found his heart filled to overflowing with the need to express the exalted mystery that had been revealed to him. How then could he keep his song from being carried along on the very wings of wonder and enthusiasm? Yet it seems certain that the author must have lived long with his inspiration, must have pondered it often in the quiet of the night, until it took fire and filled his soul with new light and realization, which he must proclaim.

My heart overflows with a goodly theme;
    as I sing my ode to the king,
    my tongue is nimble as the pen of a skill-
        ful scribe.

II

In such a spirit of wonder and admiration the
reader is first brought to contemplate the divine
Bridegroom, fairest among the sons of men. For the
inner radiance of His divinity cannot but shine
through His humanity, dazzling those who have the
will to discern it. Moreover, in His earthly life there
was always a *grace upon* His *lips* that forced even His
enemies to exclaim: "Nobody has ever spoken as this
man speaks" (John 7:46). So manifest throughout
the ages have been His words and power that it is
impossible today not to perceive in Christ's invinci-
bility the Father's approving witness: "Thou art my
beloved Son, in thee I am well pleased" (Luke 3:22).

Fairer in beauty are you than the sons of men;
    grace is poured out upon your lips;
    thus God has blessed you forever.

A Warrior-King is this divine Bridegroom, not only
fighting battles down the centuries with the mighty
weapons of *truth* and *justice*, but also bringing in as
trophies the countless victims of His love.

Gird your sword upon your thigh, O mighty
    one!
    In your splendor and your majesty ride
        on triumphant

> In the cause of truth and for the sake of
>   justice;
> and may your right hand show you
>   wondrous deeds.
> Your arrows are sharp; peoples are subject
>   to you;
> the king's enemies lose heart.

That the Bridegroom is also none other than the
Lord Himself in humble guise is attested by no less
an authority than the writer of Hebrews, who quotes
the next verses in proof of the King's divinity: "And
what [does the Father say] of the Son? Thy throne,
O God, stands firm for ever and ever; the sceptre of
thy kingship is a rod that rules true" (Heb. 1:8).
Besides, His is a just reign, enduring forever, while
He governs—though how invisibly at times!—with
a scepter of ultimate *justice*, which will outlast all
evil and subdue wickedness. For this King, the true
Anointed One, has been consecrated not by any
outward unction, such as was used of old for princes
and priests. His very divinity is the anointing poured
out upon His humanity like a sacred oil to constitute
Him High Priest and Mediator between God and
Man. Even the robes of His human nature are
redolent with the sacrificial aroma of His victimhood
signified by the death-proclaiming *myrrh* and the
aloes, a perfumed wood suggesting the redemptive
fragrance of the cross. By this, once He is raised upon
it, He draws to Himself all hearts, even the *daughters
of kings,* so that from the *ivory palaces* of the rich,
too, there may be such worship as will *bring* Him
joy. That is to say, time was when kings and queens

found leisure to pray the "Hours" of the Divine Office, as likewise today many a busy executive pays to the King of kings His meed of praise even in the marts of Mammon.

> Your throne, O God, stands forever and
>   ever;
>   a tempered rod is your royal scepter,
> You love justice and hate wickedness;
>   therefore God, your God, has anointed
>   you
>   with the oil of gladness above your fellow
>   kings.
> With myrrh and aloes and cassia your robes
>   are fragrant;
>   from ivory palaces string music brings
>   you joy.
> The daughters of kings come to meet you;
>   the queen takes her place at your right
>   hand in gold of Ophir.

III

Now the psalmist presents Christ's Bride, the Church, whom Origen depicts as saying of herself: "When I was preparing for my marriage with the King's Son, the first-born of all creation (Col. 1:15), I had the holy angels to serve me, and they gave me the Law as a betrothal gift. . . . I had prophets, too, for my servants. They told me a great deal about the Son of God, . . . so as to set me ablaze with love for Him."[1] Yet we know that when Christ came, He had

---

[1] Jean Daniélou, S.J., *Origen* (New York: Sheed and Ward, 1955), p. 119.

to ask her to leave her *father's house* and *forget* her own *people,* who had rejected Him. As often in human marriage, the Bride had to abandon all things and follow her *lord* into far-off lands and live among strangers. Origen further relates: "He called to her and asked her to leave the things of the flesh for the things of the spirit and the things she could see for the things she could not see."[1]

So also the Christian today, as he enters more and more into this mystery of the Lord's espousal to the Church—and therefore to each individual soul—hears this same plea of Christ in the depths of his own consciousness: the call to a greater detachment from the things of time. For a bride must always give herself without reserve, make a clean break with the past, and live only for the King, her Lord.

> Hear, O daughter, and see; turn your ear,
>   forget your people and your father's
>   house.
> So shall the king desire your beauty;
>   for he is your lord, and you must worship
>   him.

Sprung as she was from the mystery of the Old Testament, how richly has Christ's royal bride, the Church, been compensated for leaving the home where she was born and nurtured. Now the *city of Tyre,* symbol of all the Gentile world, attends her with priceless gifts, while the *rich* among all peoples *seek* her royal Spouse's *favor.* How sublimely true this is when one recalls the countless galaxy of saints

---

[1] *Ibid.,* pp. 143-144.

from every race and nation, all bringing to the mystic
marriage their dearest treasures—the dower of their
complete self-giving.

> And the city of Tyre is here with gifts;
>   the rich among the people seek your favor.

Now comes the Bride herself, a truly royal daugh-
ter, resplendent in holiness, her raiment adorned
beyond compare with the gems of her Bridegroom's
own matchless virtues. For now she is flesh of His
flesh; and all His riches are hers. Thus down the
centuries the virgins of her train, nation after nation,
are brought in to the heavenly Bridegroom. Rejoicing
at the "glad tidings" they have heard at long last,
they come with joy to *enter the palace of the king.*

> All glorious is the king's daughter as she
>   enters;
>   her raiment is threaded with spun gold.
> In embroidered apparel she is borne in to
>   the king;
>   behind her the virgins of her train are
>   brought to you.
> They are borne in with gladness and joy;
>   they enter the palace of the king.

IV

The poem ends with a final pledge to the Bridegroom. Christ, the Son of David whose *fathers* had
ruled but one petty kingdom in a far corner of the
world, will have by His mystical marriage *sons* who
will be spiritual *princes* over all the earth. That is
why the Church chants so fittingly the following

verses on the feasts of the apostles and evangelists,
since through them and their descendants God has
indeed made His *name memorable* even to the end
of time.

> The place of your fathers your sons shall
>   have;
>   you shall make them princes through all
>   the land.
> I will make your name memorable through
>   all generations;
>   therefore shall nations praise you forever
>   and ever.

When that *forever* of time's reckoning will have
come to an end, the mystic marriage will be consummated in a new heaven and a new earth. Then the
Church Triumphant will be "sent down by God from
heaven all clothed in readiness, like a bride who has
adorned herself to meet her husband" (Apoc. 21:2).
Then will the Bridegroom and the Bride say "Come!"
to all their retinue who have celebrated with reverence and gratitude these mystic nuptials of time,
which were but a faint foreshadowing of the eternal
wedding feast to which all are invited in the everlasting kingdom.

THIRD STEP

FROM LIFE'S NATURAL LEVEL TO NEW HEIGHTS OF COSMIC PRAISE

A person has been purged of his old self and its earth-bound desires by casting them into the abyss of divine mercy. To Christ he has been joined, not only by a communion of life-principle but also by a united purpose—that of prayer and self-immolation for the world's salvation. Now the soul is ready to pass through the gates of life-on-the-natural-level into a new universe of vastly extended horizons.

Here, where heaven and earth are one, and where Christ is all in all, Christians may actually become His heart and mind and voice, so as to join in that unceasing hymn of praise and adoration begun in heaven but now extended to the farthest reaches of earth. Wherever Christ-in-His-members may realize their highest prerogatives, they are saying with the choirs of heaven:

> Praise the Lord in his sanctuary. . . .
> Praise him for his mighty deeds, . . .
>   praise him for his sovereign majesty. . . .

Let everything that has breath praise the
Lord. Alleluia.

(Ps. 150:1, 2, 6)

Psalm 113—Every Christian Soul Has Its Exodus

A

Psalm 113, one of the Hallel used for the Paschal
Feast, must have been sung by the Savior Himself
and His Apostles at the Last Supper. And how appro-
priately! For this hymn historically commemorated
Israel's going out from Egypt and its miraculous
passing through the Red Sea to become a new people
in a new kind of existence. This same hymn at that
Supper-Sacrifice was to be the inaugural of the New
Covenant, which brought about the freeing of God's
people from the bondage of original sin by means
of their sacramental passage through the Red Sea of
Christ's redeeming death.

Ever since that sacred night the whole Church
has been going *forth from Egypt* in each individual
member, who must make the same journey, experience the same hunger and thirst, fight the same battles, know the same darkness and light, the same
struggles. For each soul, too, has to build within itself a tabernacle where God may dwell and become a
wayfarer with it in order to lead it on to its final
destination, the eternal Promised Land. This means
that Christians also have miraculous aids, of which
those given to the Jews in the desert were but a
feeble representation. Instead of manna we today
have the life-giving bread of the Eucharist; in place
of water from the rock, we may slake our spiritual

thirst with supernatural life gushing forth in the sacraments from the riven side of Christ. Just as Israel
had for final goal "a land all milk and honey" (Deut.
11:9), so Christians today know that even this era
of the redemption accomplished is not their real
Promised Land. Rather they are still in the desert
of their testing and formation, the time between their
own Exodus and the entrance into that everlasting
City where "the nations will live and move in [the]
radiance" of God's glory (Apoc. 21:24).

For these reasons Psalm 113 is saturated with the
thought of the Christian Passover and Exodus, prefigured by the historical Pasch of the Hebrews. This
is why the praise of God's glory and power are as
fresh and vivid in this poem now as three thousand
years ago. For there is something eternal about God's
revelation in history—so eternal that all other actors
in the great drama, even Moses, fade away—and the
Almighty Himself here stands forth alone as the
Great Protagonist. Even the people merge into in-
significance as but *his sanctuary, his domain.* And,
while the sea and river flee away in awe, Mount
Sinai and the surrounding hills quake at the tremendous manifestation of His will in the giving of
the law.

Such were the facts. But here the psalmist describes the event in his superb imagery. He tells us
that so great was the people's joy over the new-won
freedom that their exultation affected all surrounding nature. Therefore quaking Sinai-and its foothills
are poetically likened to sheep and lambs frolicking
in green-clad meadows, while the forbidding water

barriers respectfully draw back to make room for
God's people to cross. Then the psalmist asks, as if
in surprise, why dull matter and dumb animals so
reacted to the divine presence and power. It was
because a poet's insight could discern even in the
lower forms of creation an instinct of reverence and
awe, paradoxically mingled with irrepressible delight. For the Mighty One who could bring forth
water from hard and barren rock was also able to
thrill lowly and insentient creation with a dim recog-
nition of its Maker's power and holiness.

> When Israel came forth from Egypt,
> the house of Jacob from a people of alien
> tongue,
> Juda became his sanctuary,
> Israel his domain.
> The sea beheld and fled;
> Jordan turned back.
> The mountains skipped like rams,
> the hills like the lambs of the flock.
>
> Why is it, O sea, that you flee?
> O Jordan, that you turn back?
> You mountains, that you skip like rams?
> You hills, like the lambs of the flock?
>
> Before the face of the Lord, tremble, O
> earth,
> before the face of the God of Jacob,
> Who turned the rock into pools of water,
> the flint into flowing springs.

B-I

Scarcely had the Israelites begun their new life
when, forgetting the hardships of their former slavery, they remembered only the "bowls of meat" in
Egypt and "more bread than we needed to content
us" (Ex. 16:3). The Promised Land being a whole
desert of hardships away, they longed only for the
abandoned satisfactions of the old life. This is a
figure of what frequently happens to God's people
today, who, after crossing the Red Sea of their baptism or its paschal renewal, often yearningly revert
to the fleshpots of the old life of pleasure and world-
liness. Even the human element of the Church at
times becomes so entangled outwardly with the
cross-purposes of wealth and earthly ambition that
we have heard the scoffers asking, *"Where is their
God?* Christianity has failed!" Of course, Chester-
ton's answer still stands: Christianity has never been
tried—except by the saints and the relatively few
who have rightly attributed the success of their efforts not to themselves but to God. These know only
too well, however, that although the Lord may do
whatever he wills, He has nevertheless endowed man
with the terrifying power of casting up even to
heaven his defiant cry: "Not Thy will but mine be
done!"

> Not to us, O Lord, not to us
>   but to your name give glory
>   because of your kindness, because of your
>   truth.
> Why should the pagans say,
>   "Where is their God?"

Our God is in heaven;
   whatever he wills, he does.

II

The Israelites, as they passed among the desert tribes and observed their idolatry, made smug comparisons between dead idols and their own living God, comparisons unwarranted by the Israelites' subsequent behavior. So also we in the modern world, while feeling disdain for persons who actually worship figures of wood or metal, may do well first to examine the objects of our own current cults; such, for example, the "popular personality," too often a sports figure or a Hollywood celebrity—or perhaps even a scientist, whose fame seemingly entitles him to a hearing even when he chooses to make pronouncements on some moral or religious issue. Favorite speakers and politicians, too, have their incense-burning shrines, if they can stir up enough hysteria or else suggest an easy panacea for the world's present ills. For all such petty deities the psalmist offers a touchstone to test their intrinsic worth.

They have eyes. But can they *see* to penetrate beneath the outward surface of things to the profound realities actually involved, to the hidden forces shaping the world's destinies? Do they *hear* only the acclaim of the crowd, or can they heed the still, small voice of God either in their own heart or in the wiser voices of the intelligent few motivated not by emotion but by calm reason? Can they *feel* the things of the spirit, so as to find beneath the color of the skin, the foreign accent, or the manners of an exotic culture, the common brotherhood and human dignity of every man?

One can thus wisely test all the idols generally worshipped today, whether these be demagogues or ideas whose cult they have promoted. The latter would signify anything one is prone to put in God's place as the supreme good, if it were only for a momentary pleasure. So the psalmist warns, while all idols are blind and deaf and unfeeling, they nevertheless have one momentous effect on their devotees. What they admire they unconsciously tend to emulate. Therefore any man who fashions for himself idols out of his own self-ideal or mob hysteria *shall* inevitably come to *be like them*.

> Their idols are silver and gold,
>   the handiwork of men.
> They have mouths but speak not;
>   they have eyes but see not;
> They have ears but hear not;
>   they have noses but smell not;
> They have hands but feel not;
>   they have feet but walk not;
>   they utter no sound from their throat.
> Their makers shall be like them,
>   everyone that trusts in them.

III

Even after Israel had entered the Promised Land, its longed-for goal, the stark reality of many circumstances soon proved that this was but a figurative end to their pilgrimage. And so, even as the people continued to sing this psalm in thanksgiving for their historical exodus, they gradually came to recall that wondrous experience as but the basis and pledge for some future mysterious event in which the vague figure of a New Moses would accomplish their lasting deliverance into a promised land truly abounding in unending happiness.

Likewise, modern Christians know from grim experience that even though Christ has led them through the Red Sea of baptism into a Church flowing with all spiritual delights, nevertheless they here "have no permanent city" (Heb. 13:14).[1] They too possess a Messianic hope, which perceives even in the great deeds the Savior has already accomplished a "sacrament" or heralding figure of the final act that will truly complete their deliverance thus begun. That is to say, after this New Israel, the Church, has also been tested in the desert of tribulation, the faithful "remnant" will come to yet another sea, "a sea of glass, tinged with fire." And the author of the Apocalypse, tying up the threads of history and prophecy, tells us: "And by this sea of glass the victors were standing, safe now from the beast. . . . Theirs is the song of God's servant Moses," as they exult in their final escape from an oppressive Pharaoh and make ready now to hymn God's praises everlastingly (Apoc. 15:2-3).

Such is the final justification for the attitude of confidence and gratitude that pervades the last verses of this psalm. Bringing together into one glad refrain the *trust* of all baptized Christians, especially members of the ordained priesthood, it all-inclusively

---

[1] Confraternity of Christian Doctrine translation.

names likewise *those who fear the Lord;* i.e., non-Catholics who are in a state of grace by reason of their faith and baptism of desire. The Lord remembers and blesses all.

> The house of Israel trusts in the Lord;
>   he is their help and their shield.
> The house of Aaron trusts in the Lord;
>   he is their help and their shield.
> Those who fear the Lord trust in the Lord;
>   he is their help and their shield.
> The Lord remembers us and will bless us:
>   he will bless the house of Israel;
>   he will bless the house of Aaron;
> He will bless those who fear the Lord,
>   both the small and the great.
> May the Lord bless you more and more,
>   both you and your children.
> May you be blessed by the Lord,
>   who made heaven and earth.

At length the Christian, as he stands in spirit on the final threshold of that crystal sea, pauses to evoke praise from the three realms of existence, "so that everything in heaven and on earth and under the earth must bend the knee before the name of Jesus, and every tongue must confess Jesus Christ as the Lord, dwelling in the glory of God the Father" (Phil. 2:10-11). *The heaven of the Lord* already has its "thousands of thousands, . . . crying aloud, Power, and God-head, wisdom and strength, honour and glory, and blessing are his by right, the Lamb that was slain" (Apoc. 5:11-12). As to earth, God has placed that under man's dominion, that he need not offer forced service but should so use all creatures as to

make of them a continual sacrifice of praise and
thanksgiving. Those, however, who are *dead* in
mortal sin can praise the Lord no more than they who
have already sunk into the morass of that eternal
silence, to which their defiance of His love has
brought them. Dante understood this well when he
placed on the lips of souls entering Purgatory this
beautiful psalm of the Exodus. But he had no song at
all for the dismal company of the damned.

> Heaven is the heaven of the Lord,
>> but the earth he has given to the children
>> of men.
> It is not the dead who praise the Lord,
>> nor those who go down into silence.

Finally, as if to remind all those now living that
"the day of salvation has come already" (II Cor. 6:3),
the psalmist climaxes his long exodus of the spirit
from Egypt to the shores of eternity with this ex-
clamation summing up all that any soul can do here
and now in its desert testing:

> But we [who live] bless the Lord,
>> both now and forever.

Psalm 62—Glimpse of the Promised Land from the Desert

This psalm has a surprisingly modern ring, since
it assumes that souls of every epoch, dispersed over
a multitude of even worthy interests and pursuits,
must sometimes become aware of a certain emptiness
which none but God can fill. Even with the best intentions men inevitably find their thoughts and desires lured away from "the one thing necessary" to

become "careful and troubled" about many things, such as their work and ambitions, the people they deal with, or even public events they cannot sway. They ought often, then, to be aware of the need for moments of recollection, in order to re-establish in the depth of their souls that dynamic unity of purpose which alone can give meaning to their own manifold activities. How beautifully Psalm 62 enables them to do just this, by framing from out the superficiality of myriad distractions a fervent appeal to the only One for whom all hearts were made. Depicting the soul as a parched wilderness, drained of all productivity, the first verse makes a person realize his utter thirst for the refreshing water of divine life, which is so essential for complete living that even his *flesh pines* for it.

> O God, you are my God whom I seek;
>   for you my flesh pines and my soul thirsts
>   like the earth, parched, lifeless and with-
>   out water.

But there is little use of God's grace moistening souls while they are busy thoroughfares wide open to the constant trafficking of earth-bent enterprises. This is why the psalm suggests that a man must now and then withdraw, at least in mind, to that *sanctuary* where "The loud vociferations of the street/ Become an indistinguishable roar."[1] This, of course, is that "inner room" of one's own secret self where, regardless of his surroundings, he can be alone with God. Here the soul may not only speak face to face with

---

[1] Henry Wadsworth Longfellow, *"Sonnet on the Divine Comedy."*

its Lord, but also it may alert the heart to listen, so as to accept whatever light or spiritual impulse He may give it. This could be an actual grace to do some specific thing or to accept a certain sacrifice His love demands. Or else such a light could consist of a deeper insight into God's very nature, a revelation that will draw the soul closer to Him in a more steadfast union.

> Thus have I gazed toward you in the sanctuary
>   to see your power and your glory,
> For your kindness is a greater good than life;
>   my lips shall glorify you.

Such special gifts are not had for the mere asking, however; they usually must be earned by an ardent longing born of prayer. This is why the psalmist says that even when a person experiences no sensible satisfaction, when he feels most discouraged about his spiritual life, he must nevertheless persevere and continue to *call upon* God's *name*. Just as the priest at Mass holds up his hands to express by a bodily gesture the longing of his spirit, Christians also must lift up the two powers of their soul—their will and understanding—toward Him who alone can satisfy their indefinable yearning.

> Thus will I bless you while I live;
>   lifting up my hands, I will call upon your name.

A wonderful transformation can be wrought by such ardent and persevering prayer. Although beginners in the spiritual life once hungered for emotional satisfaction, they may now find their souls strangely filled with an indescribable new kind of happiness, one that transcends all earthly experience. This will probably take the form of only occasional nibbles of delight, for their souls could not sustain a prolonged joy of this kind. Moreover, they will find that their prayer has somehow passed beyond the customary litany of petitions to a spontaneous adoration prompted by the discovery of the infinite treasures of that beauty and truth they were privileged to glimpse.

> As with the riches of a banquet shall my soul
>   be satisfied,
>   and with exultant lips my mouth shall
>   praise you.

Next the psalmist assumes that such souls have been sufficiently enamored by the fleeting vision of infinite Goodness to endeavor to make It the center as well as the goal of their waking life. To this end the next verse suggests that they use the spacious moments of the night and dawn, before the inrush of the day's activities, to focus their mind and heart on God. The result of that effort would be such a reward as only a divine generosity could devise. So the psalmist assumes that souls are truly endeavoring to prepare for God's visitation of grace by surrendering unconditionally to His will beneath the wings of His compassionate love. Thereupon He may fill such generous ones even here and now with carefree trust in His Providence—a trust which brings with it the kind of joy that nothing on earth can quench.

I will remember you upon my couch,
    and through the night-watches I will
       meditate on you:
That you are my help,
    and in the shadow of your wings I shout
       for joy.
My soul clings fast to you;
    your right hand upholds me.

From this vantage point of God's sheltering arms we may also anticipate our triumph over any habits or passions that have formerly wrecked our best resolves. Such forces of lower nature are already potentially vanquished by the very fact of our surrender to God's will. Lest, however, those evils revive and plague us with renewed attacks, we now give them over to the *sword* of self-denial and consign them to the contemptible grave of a dead and buried past.

But they shall be destroyed who seek my
       life,
    they shall go into the depths of the earth;
They shall be delivered over to the sword,
    and shall be the prey of jackals.

With this anticipation of victory divinely given, the curtains of eternity part ever so slightly, so that Christ's battle-scarred members may have a fleeting glimpse of their triumphal home-coming. Now they can see that, while traitorous souls will be silenced in eternal darkness, there will be exultant joy for all who, having sworn allegiance to the King, have kept their honor untarnished in the fray.

The king, however, shall rejoice in God;
everyone who swears by him shall glory,
but the mouths of those who speak falsely
shall be stopped.

Psalm 83—Longing for God Is the Soul's Homage

Once a person, by allowing himself to be stripped
of all the unrealities this world has to offer, has entered with Christ into His redeeming death—once
that person has experienced the darkness and accepted it creatively, then his soul is ready to rise with
the Redeemer into a new life made possible through
His glorious resurrection. In other words, those who
are Christ's now give free play to the gift which
endows them with a spiritual taste, a relish for the
things of God, the supernatural gift of wisdom. Far
from being a merely sensible devotion, this is a true
experience of what is divine, since it makes the soul
instinctively long for God's presence in preference
to any joys of earth. This is what St. Paul had in mind
when he wrote: "Risen, then, with Christ, you must
lift your thoughts above, where Christ now sits at
the right hand of God. You must be heavenly-minded,
not earthly minded" (Col. 3:1-3).

To voice the longing proper to this new kind of
supernatural existence the Church uses the same
tender hymn sung by the ancient Jews to express
their homesickness for the temple of Jerusalem. That
was the earthly dwelling place of God, symbol not
only of His Church on earth but also of the heavenly
Jerusalem, the City where the Lord Almighty is Himself the temple (Apoc. 21:22). When the Christian

thinks, then, of this, the ultimate aim of his earthly
pilgrimage, he may well exclaim in faith and longing:

> How lovely is your dwelling place,
> O Lord of hosts!

If even God's earthly tabernacle, the place of His
Eucharistic presence, can sometimes fill the soul with
a sense of peace to be found nowhere else on earth,
what must be the rapture of those celestial courts,
man's final goal for all eternity? Wherefore, then,
should Christians not often "lift [their] thoughts
above" and so find their hearts gravitating toward
that eternal destination with all the homing instinct
of a bird that wings its way unerringly through storm
and danger to the warm shelter of its own nest? In
fact, one's whole being, *heart* and *flesh*, keenly aware
of the hazards lurking everywhere in any apartness
from God, ought to *yearn* with an unspeakable sense
of need for the peace and safety of His presence.

> My soul yearns and pines
>   for the courts of the Lord.
> My heart and my flesh
>   cry out for the living God.
> Even the sparrow finds a home,
>   and the swallow a nest
>   in which she puts her young—
> Your altars, O Lord of hosts,
>   my king and my God!

Happy are they who have already reached their
goal and are living the rapturous life of adoration,
bathed in the light of the beatific vision. But even
here in the midst of this earthly exile Christians may

enjoy a wondrous happiness, provided their *hearts are set* steadfastly on the end of the pilgrimage. For then they can say with St. Paul: "Nothing is beyond my powers, thanks to the strength God gives me" (Phil. 4:13).

> Happy they who dwell in your house!
> continually they praise you.
> Happy the men whose strength you are!
> their hearts are set upon the pilgrimage.

As those who were deified[1] in baptism *pass through the arid valley* of this life, with all its barren material pursuits and purposes, they may find that their own souls, even though parched and dry for want of emotional satisfaction, can be the instruments by which the desert land is changed into a place of springs. That is because God often chooses such means for giving His living water to other souls that are dry and cynical and self-absorbed. If, then, Christians will but live the mystery of their redemption by surrendering themselves to the Father with Christ and by loving others for His sake, it is possible that even now the *arid valley* of their own environment may drink in the *early rain* of redeeming grace and be clothed with the generous growth of a new creation. Consequently, they who would be apostles in their own milieu may thus take on fresh moral strength until, no longer blinded by any mists of worldly values, they arrive at a whole new vision of truth. This will enable them to see even now with the eyes of faith

---

[1] Jean Daniélou, S.J., *The Lord of History* (Chicago: Henry Regnery Company, 1958) p. 192.

the God who abides in Sion, His Church of earth and
heaven.

> When they pass through the arid valley,
>   they make a spring of it;
>   the early rain clothes it with generous
>   growth.
> They go from strength to strength;
>   they shall see the God of gods in Sion.

Such consummation of man's Godwardness is so
devoutly to be wished that all may now beseech the
Lord to make them utilize to the full the life-sharing
power of their own steadfast faith. Thus they may
help to vitalize by it a whole new mode of living for
themselves and others.

> O Lord of hosts, hear my prayer;
>   Hearken, O God of Jacob!
> O God, behold our shield [Christ, our Pro-
>   tector],
>   and look upon the face of your anointed.

For all who have been *anointed* with the new Christ-
life can cry with the beloved Son, "Abba, Father"
(Rom. 8:15).

In this modern era especially, there is always
danger that Christians may be carried away by the
spirit of activism. Here then is an inspired message
for all who are so involved in sundry activities that
they no longer find time to pray. The psalmist reminds them that *one day* of prayer is in God's sight
worth *a thousand* spent in action spurred on by only
natural enthusiasm; that the humble soul who makes
itself a mendicant at the Lord's door is doing more

for His glory than the popular leader who draws crowds by nothing more than his natural charm and personality.

> I had rather one day in your courts
> than a thousand elsewhere;
> I had rather lie at the threshold of the house
> of my God
> than dwell in the tents of the wicked.

Only in God's presence does a soul find the real source of all the things for which its innermost being yearns incessantly. That is to say, the Lord is its *sun* and *shield,* since from Him comes an ever-flowing spring of light as well as sure protection. St. Paul glowingly exclaimed to the worldly-wise Corinthians: "Eye has not seen nor ear heard, nor has it entered into the heart of man" to conceive the greatness of the grace and glory which "God has prepared for those who love him" (I Cor. 2:9).[1] Such is His love that He cannot withhold any gift, provided only the soul seek Him *in sincerity.*

> For a sun and a shield is the Lord God;
> grace and glory he bestows;
> The Lord withholds no good thing
> from those who walk in sincerity.

During life's long pilgrimage through the arid valley of the spiritual way, a person sometimes finds himself bereft of human consolation before he has reached the spring of divine comfort. Then he may remember it is a maxim of the Christian life that the

---

[1] Confraternity of Christian Doctrine translation.

soul must first leave all before it can find all in God. Therefore any Christian, putting his hand confidingly into Christ's, should learn to exclaim with complete abandonment as he goes forward into the blinding mist of the unknown:

> O Lord of hosts,
>   happy the men who trust in you!

Psalm 94—The Holy Spirit Invites All to Adore

This psalm is used daily in every form of Office as an invitation from the Holy Spirit Himself for all men to come and adore the Lord. Acting as a prelude to the whole Divine Office, this beautiful hymn is like the Introit of the Mass, which announces the mood and occasion of the feast being celebrated. That is, this psalm, with the antiphon of the season or festival interspersed between its verses, clearly sets the keynote for the day. In this manner the souls who so pray, although still conscious of their condition as creatures, are enabled to share in spirit and grace each event of that vast redeeming work which the Word came down upon earth to accomplish. Thus through all the Invitatories of the year, from Christmas through Easter to Pentecost, amid sorrow for sins and negligences, Christians may enter, heart and mind, with Christ into His self-abasement and trials, even to the sharing in His triumph. All these mysteries are relived with Him in full cognizance that they who take the inspired word on their lips have an actual part with and through Him in the wondrous work of redemption being wrought *today*.

Come, let us sing joyfully to the Lord;
    let us acclaim the Rock of our salvation.
Let us greet him with thanksgiving;
    let us joyfully sing psalms to him.

The Holy Spirit next reveals the fundamental reason for this call to worship God: He is the fullness of all being, *far above all gods*. This means He is above anything that could possibly be represented as deserving of man's homage. Infinitely self-sufficient, He nevertheless chose to create humanity by a mere movement of love and then gave it the universe as its temple of worship.

For the Lord is a great God,
    and a great king above all gods;
In his hands are the depths of the earth,
    and the tops of the mountains are his.
His is the sea, for he has made it,
    and the dry land, which his hands have
        formed.

When intelligent creatures contemplate in its measureless depths and heights the majesty of the sea and the immensity of the land—the works of His hands—what other words should burst forth from the wells of their being except these: "Come, let us adore"?

Come, let us bow down in worship;
    let us kneel before the Lord who made
    us.

Prostrate thus in adoration, those who pray with heart as well as lips are now enabled to see further depths of divine reality, finding in the Omnipotent not a distant divinity but *our* God. This infinite Deity so loved the world that He sent His only-begotten Son as a lowly Shepherd to seek and guide His sheep which are ever wandering astray.

> For he is our God,
>   and we are the people he shepherds,
>   the flock he guides.

So great was His love and solicitude that He has recorded for all peoples a prophetic warning, applied first to the Israelites in the desert, yet valid still for the modern world. *Today* is that momentous now —that "day of salvation" given everyone to work out his eternal destiny. Sometimes *today* may be a new supernatural light bestowed by Christ on a particular feast. Or else *today* may be a signal grace for true conversion of heart, if only one will *hear his voice* speaking through the liturgy, a sermon or book, or even through some inner urge uttered only in the heart.

The important thing is not to be insensitive to the divine call through indifference or lack of confidence in the means that may have been chosen. For *Meriba* stands as a lasting monument to God's avenging wrath on those who had rebelled against the instruments of His guidance. And *Massa* is the symbol of shame in those who withheld their trust from Him, although He had already manifested His power in the marvels of the Exodus.

> Oh, that today you would hear his voice:
>   "Harden not your hearts as at Meriba,

> as in the day of Massa in the desert,
> Where your fathers tempted me;
>   they tested me though they had seen my
>   works."

How careful, then, one must be to guard against any like neglect of God or forgetfulness of His omnipotence today. For even the Lord of love can turn away in detestation from those who persistently reject His grace and ignore His manifest will.

> "Forty years I loathed that generation,
>   and I said: They are a people of erring
>   heart,
>   and they know not my ways.
> Therefore I swore in my anger:
>   they shall not enter into my rest."

A terrifying thought!—to be thus abandoned by the Creator with an oath of eternal condemnation. For the *rest* of which He speaks is nothing else but that true Sabbath attained only in the life beyond death, when the soul, freed from bodily works, will be wholly absorbed in divine contemplation. This means a sharing in God's own rest, that everlasting Sabbath where His own will take part forever in the marriage feast of the Lamb.

Psalm 112—High Flight on the Wings of Faith and Love

Psalm 112, fourth of the vesper hymns for the Lord's own day, is especially dear to the Church because of its association with the Last Supper and Christ's supreme gift of the Eucharist. This psalm, one of the Hallel sung at the paschal meal, belonged

to the ritual preceding the final chalice over which
Jesus said the memorable words, "This is my blood."
Christians today may use the same sacred hymn to
pay their own tribute of praise to the All-Holy for
His exaltation in the great mystery of redeeming
love.

> Praise, you servants of the Lord,
>   praise the name of the Lord.
> Blessed be the name of the Lord
>   both now and forever.
> From the rising to the setting of the sun
>   is the name of the Lord to be praised.

How ought that *name* to be praised today? Surely
not by mere lip service! Rather should Christians
make it their first object of reverence and adoration,
since God's *name* embodies His very nature; and
therefore the Lord Himself has entered into it as His
earthly dwelling place. We know this because He
thus testified after the consecration of the ancient
temple: "My name shall be there" (III Kings 8:29),[1]
signifying His personal abiding. And so when we today praise this *name* in reverence and devotion, we
may find our whole being also enwrapped by His
presence as by the cloud which "wreathed the Lord's
house with His own glory" (*ibid.* 8:10-12). Then, if
we surrender to this all-encompassing power, we may
feel it even penetrate our innermost life, and so raise
us to a new level of thought and insight.

All this could mean that, like a young poet-aviator
in the war, when we pray this psalm we may also slip
for a time "the surly bonds of earth, / . . . Up, up the

---

[1] Douai Version.

long, delirious, burning blue" we may soar and top
"the wind-swept heights . . ., /Where never lark, or
even eagle flew. /And while with silent, lifting mind
trod /The high untrespassed sanctity of space, /[we
too may] put out [our] hand" and touch with living
faith "the face of God."[1] Such is the wondrous spiritual experience that the ancient psalmist seems to
have expressed in his inspired poem. He who never
dreamed that man would some day surpass the eagle
in flight, had already in spirit "soared and swung /
High in the sunlit silence" to commune alone with
Him who makes the clouds His chariot and mounts
on the wings of the wind (Ps. 103:3). And so in this
modern world of marvels—whether rapt in wonder
while in actual flight, or raised in spirit on the pinions
of this prayer—each of us may say with true meaning
and conviction, "I have put out my hand and touched
the face of God!"

> High above all nations is the Lord;
>   above the heavens is his glory.
> Who is like the Lord, our God, who is
>   enthroned on high
>   and looks upon the heavens and the earth
>   below?

But how can we mere mortals, without special
light of divine inspiration, mount on the wings of
such a prayer as this, which carries us spiritually
far beyond the reaches of human thought and imagination? Love alone can bear a person beyond the earth-
bound limitations of his intellect and so enable him
to penetrate into the mystery of God's own being.

---
1 Pilot Officer John Gillespie Magee, *"High Flight."*

There he will discover in the Trinity of the three divine Persons an infinite giving of life. This wells over through the Incarnation to embrace all mankind in a oneness of charity "poured out in our hearts by the Holy Spirit" (Rom. 5:5). By means of this inspired psalm, then, the soul could with love find itself caught up in that same circuit of mutual giving, which comprises the very life of the Triune God. For we know that

> He raises up the lowly from the dust;
> from the dunghill he lifts up the poor
> To seat them with princes,
> with the princes of his own people.

Now a person can begin to grasp the meaning of the psalm's last verse. God has indeed taken the *barren wife*, [unredeemed humanity], and established her in the *home* of His innermost life. There, deified by the Father's adoption, she can continually bring forth offspring at the baptismal font of the new creation wrought by Christ's redeeming love.

> He establishes in her home the barren wife
> as the joyful mother of children.

Psalm 99—*The Source of True Happiness*

The Church has shown great wisdom and insight in appointing this psalm for her office of Lauds on feast days. For thus Christians may enter into the spirit of each festival with a gladness that will open their hearts to receive all the graces that the mystery to be celebrated can impart.

It is well known, of course, that God has prepared for all men an eternity of such delight that, while

they ever continue to explore the depths of the beatific vision, they will be lost more and more in never-
ending amazement and rapture. Yet even in this
earthly life the man of faith can discover that the
true source of all joy consists in the simple fact that
the Lord is God. That is to say, merely to think about
this infinite Being and His marvelous attributes can
mean to catch even now in the mirror of one's intellect some of the unquenchable joy radiating from
His immeasurable divine bliss. This is the wondrous
purpose Psalm 99 may serve when it invites all men
the world over, in the Office or in private prayer to

> Sing joyfully to the Lord, all you lands;
>   serve the Lord with gladness;
>   come before him with joyful song.
> Know that the Lord is God;
>   he made us, his we are;
>   his people, the flock he tends.

But such delight does not happen automatically.
A person must first endeavor to focus his mind on
God. Just as a looking glass has to be set properly
in order to reflect the splendor of the sun, so the
soul has to be fully turned toward God in interest and
intent, if it is to catch the effulgence of His joy. Yet
how often men are oriented, instead, toward the
things of this world, reflecting only their own self-
esteem or seeking to bask in the light of others' admiration. That is why St. Paul urges all Christians:
"You must lift your thoughts above" (Col. 3:1).

So far one's own self-knowledge and efforts may
reach. Now the psalm takes over and leads Christians through the *gates* of their natural perspective
into the *courts* of that supernatural realm opened by

baptism, where they were given a life bathed in the radiance of divine light. Here, grafted on to Christ, their souls will be able to see all things from the new angle of His point of view. They will even be impregnated anew with His divine energy to do Christthings. Foremost of these is to carry on the work which He deemed paramount: offering the homage of creation to its Maker. For this purpose the Savior always used His human body on earth as a sacred temple of worship. For this He would still make His Mystical Body the instrument for pouring forth to the Father such hymns of praise and thanks as are due to the infinite majesty of the Godhead. This is the real reason why all Christians should now

> Enter his gates with thanksgiving,
>   his courts with praise; [in order to]
> Give thanks to him; bless his name.

Here at last in the light of supernatural faith, with mind and heart raised above all earthly attractions, souls may contemplate God as He actually is, because through the inspired psalm they see Him reflected in all His splendor. That is to say, *good* to every lowly creature, *kind* even to His enemies, and so dependable in His promises that men are prone to take His faithfulness for granted, as they do the sunlight and the air they breathe.

> For he is good:
> the Lord, whose kindness endures forever,
>   and his faithfulness, to all generations.

How can such considerations as those above bring a Christian true happiness? Whenever he thus mounts on the wings of faith and prayer, he leaves the storms of life far below. Like an airplane flying above the clouds under the clear sun, he may soar in spirit up into the light of God's eternal truth. From there the murky twilight of everyday living appears as unrelated to ultimate reality as the shadow of the plane upon the luminous clouds below. Not that one can always maintain such an eminent viewpoint, any more than the plane can stay aloft forever. But this is where the psalms of praise come in. By frequently using them, fervent Christians can keep their hearts and minds so elevated above ephemeral things as to reflect the rays of God's reality on everything that happens in their life. Thus they will be enabled always to see things as they actually are, mirrored in His light who is not only Truth but also the Fountainhead of all joy.

Psalm 23—The King of Glory Enthroned

This psalm was originally composed by King David to accompany the Ark from its long wanderings through desert and battlefield into a place of honor in the city of Jerusalem. The Ark, being the most sacred symbol of God's abiding presence among His people, was looked upon as the very throne of their invisible King. Christians, however, being of the New Covenant, have always used this same beautiful hymn to celebrate in spirit the eternal reality of which that ancient procession with the Ark was but a dim prefigure. That is, those who are Christ's now hail the ascension of their Savior-King into the sanctuary of the heavenly Jerusalem, where He reigns for ever in sovereign majesty. Such is the faith which St. Paul thus confidently expressed to the Ephesians: "Measure it [his surpassing virtue] by that mighty exercise of power which he shewed when he raised Christ from the dead, and bade him sit on his right hand above the heavens, high above all princedoms . . . and every name that is known, not in this world only, but in the world to come" (Eph. 1:20-21). And so Christians in this modern era may pray the same inspired words of the psalmist, while they voice their praise and admiration of the Lord's absolute power and world dominion. Even though men today may smile at ancient Hebrew cosmogony, which believed that God had made the earth to rest on water, they must for even better reasons bow in reverence before His greatness who could set so firm a world, with its myriad laws and purposes, on so unstable a basis as the waters of man's inconstancy.

> The Lord's are the earth and its fullness;
>   the world and those who dwell in it.
> For he founded it upon the seas
>   and established it upon the rivers.

Naturally the question now arises: What mere mortal can approach such august majesty? Who— even in this age little given to reverential awe— would dare hope to enter even in mind that *holy place* where Christ triumphant now sits enthroned? St. Paul offered an answer to this query in a continuation of the letter quoted above: "And [God] made him [Christ] the head to which the whole Church is joined, so that the Church is his body" (*ibid.* 1:22-23). But where the Head is the whole body belongs. That is, provided its *hands* or actions are in conformity with the Head's directives, and its *heart*, being *clean*, is set not on vain and passing things but on those that are lasting. Such members of Christ do receive even in this world the *blessing* of a share in His very life. Moreover, those who seek on earth His *face*, even though thorn-crowned with human misery, will be rewarded by the vision of God, which constitutes the inconceivable joys of heaven.

> Who can ascend the mountain of the Lord?
> or who may stand in his holy place?
> He whose hands are sinless, whose heart is
>   clean,
>   who desires not what is vain,
>   nor swears deceitfully to his neighbor.
> He shall receive a blessing from the Lord,
>   a reward from God his savior.
> Such is the race that seeks for him,
>   that seeks the face of the God of Jacob.

The last strophe of the psalm has been interpreted by the ancient Fathers as offering a foretaste of the heavenly vision to which Christians dare aspire. The ensuing dialogue is then construed as carried on between the celestial choirs passed by the Savior in His glorious ascension. "The angels of the Lord who followed Him on earth [in His Incarnation], saw Him ascend and announced Him to the heavenly powers so that they would open their gates. The powers were in astonishment at seeing Him in the flesh," "clothed with the poor tunic of our nature, since His garments are red from the wine-press of human evils."[1] This prevented His being recognized by the heavenly choirs at the time of the ascension.

---

[1] SS. Athanasius and Gregory of Nyssa, quoted by Jean Daniélou, S.J., *The Bible and the Liturgy* (South Bend, Ind., University of Notre Dame Press, 1956), pp. 306-307.

And so "they cried out, 'Who is He?' astounded at the amazing economy of God's providence. And the angels ascending with Christ answered them: 'The Lord of powers, He is the King of glory!' "[1] Thus was taught even in heaven the great mystery that He who "dispossessed himself, and took the nature of a slave . . . and then . . . accepted an obedience which brought him to death, death on a cross"—He, and no other, is the King of Glory whom men and angels now adore (Phil. 2:7-8).

> Lift up, O gates, your lintels;
>   reach up, you ancient portals,
>   that the king of glory may come in!
> Who is this king of glory?
>   The Lord, strong and mighty,
>   the Lord, mighty in battle.
> Lift up, O gates, your lintels;
>   reach up, you ancient portals,
>   that the king of glory may come in!
> Who is this king of glory?
>   The Lord of hosts; he is the king of glory.

Psalm 66—Praise for a Bountiful Harvest of Souls

This ancient harvest hymn of thanksgiving has far deeper meaning for men of the New Dispensation, since the natural blessings of earth's fruitfulness were but types of the far greater favors that Christians enjoy in this era of redemption. Now the world, impregnated by the precious Blood of Calvary and nurtured to fruition by the warmth of the Pentecostal

---

[1] *Ibid.,* p. 306.

fire, has borne an inconceivable harvest of spiritual benedictions.

I

This psalm is so truly a hymn of praise that the Church always uses it in her Hour of Lauds. In the Roman and Short Breviary it occurs on Tuesday; in the monastic office it is sung every day to begin the morning hour of adoration. One reason for the special fondness for this particular psalm may lie in the fact that it opens with the very words of the ancient priestly blessing dictated by God Himself to Moses and daily repeated by the chosen people all through the long centuries of their waiting: "The Lord bless thee, and keep thee; the Lord smile on thee . . ." (Num. 6:24-25). The Church, however, would now have Christians pray these sacred words to ask for those same favors applied to the spiritual order: 1) to obtain God's care and protecting presence for all, 2) to experience that sense of peace which comes only when the radiance of His *face* is discerned in the glory of His will made manifest and obeyed.

> May God have pity on us and bless us;
> may he let his face shine upon us.

Moreover, one must not lose sight of the universality expressed in this prayer, since the psalmist adds to those ancient blessings a petition that all the world may know God's goodness to His people. For St. Augustine[1] boldly interprets *way* and *salvation* as meaning Christ Himself, who declared, "I am the

---

[1] St. Augustine, *Sermons for Christmas and Epiphany* (Westminster, Md., Newman, 1952).

way" (John 14:6). And the great Doctor also recalls Blessed Simeon's joyous canticle when, looking upon His God enfleshed, he sang: "Now thou dost dismiss thy servant, O Lord, /according to thy word, in peace; /Because my eyes have seen thy salvation, . . . A light of revelation to the Gentiles" (Luke 2:29-32).[1]

> So may your way be known upon earth;
> among all nations, your salvation,
> [dwelling spiritually in His Church on
> earth].

Thus praise itself becomes a kind of apostolate, since he who so worships would by his action of giving grateful thanks draw others' attention to the object of his own devotion, that they also may learn to know and love his God. When in eternity men come to discover the amazing secret ways of grace, how many conversions will be found to have been wrought by unbelievers' having attended a Divine Office in church or monastery and there experiencing a Damascus Road where Christ was waiting to overwhelm them with His grace. It so happened to Ignace Lepp, as he has testified in his book, *From Karl Marx to Jesus Christ*.[2]

> May the peoples praise you, O God;
> may all the peoples praise you!

II

The second strophe is a direct prayer for the conversion of all nations—that they may come to know

---

1 Confraternity of Christian Doctrine translation.
2 New York: Sheed and Ward, 1959.

the God who already rules their destinies. For His guidance is so right in all it decrees that even the heathen should be led by natural reason and grace to embrace the joy and happiness found in His justness.

> May the nations be glad and exult
> > because you rule the peoples in equity;
> > the nations on the earth you guide.
> > May the peoples praise you, O God;
> > May all the peoples praise you!

III

Every Christian has a divine vocation to nurture in each human heart the Christ-life bestowed in baptism. For the Lord Himself has implanted in the world His kingdom as a tiny grain of mustard seed, which must be carefully cultivated until it grows into a great tree that fills all the earth. How truly then is this next verse fulfilled in the unceasing harvest of souls:

> The earth has yielded its fruits;
> God, our God, has blessed us.

That all may have the light and strength and courage for such an apostolate is the next petition:

> May God bless us!

Then, while one strives with all his might to extend Christ's kingdom, he likewise must pray that God Himself may give the increase, since without Him human efforts can avail nothing at all.

And may all the ends of the earth fear him!

Psalm 133—Heavenly Sentinels on Night Watch

This lovely good-night hymn is always used by the Church in her Compline for Sundays and feasts. The monastic office, however, has adopted it for every evening with the same purpose for which any Christian—monk or layman—might well bring to a close his day of endeavoring to live completely out of himself in Christ. Here, then, at day's end, when human frailty must seek repose, the Christian commits to the choirs of heaven the charge of prolonging God's praise through the watches of the night, as he exhorts them:

> Come, bless the Lord,
>   all you servants of the Lord
> Who stand in the house of the Lord
>   during the hours of the night.
> Lift up your hands toward the sanctuary,
>   and bless the Lord.

Thereupon comes the reply from those who dwell in heaven's courts, conveying to souls on earth the nightly blessing of Him who made all things in love and who wills them to take their needed rest.

> May the Lord bless you from Sion,
>   the maker of heaven and earth.

Psalm 95—New Song for a New Creation

When David brought the Ark of God's presence into the tabernacle prepared for it in Jerusalem, he

bade the people sing a *new song* to celebrate the bour-
geoning of a new era in Israel's history. Yet that
earthly Jerusalem, the place of the Lord's enthrone-
ment, was only a figure of the really new creation
amid which Christians are living now, where the
Word of God dwells among us in His ever-redeeming
Mystery. Herein He fulfills the purpose of His own
passage from death to life by ever forming a new
Israel, which, by the abandonment of its old and
natural mode of existence, is always passing into the
continuous mystery of its own transfiguration in
Christ.

This is why far more than the Israelites of old,
Christians ought *to sing a new song,* since their praise
must ever be enriched from day to day by new inner
experience, a new depth of knowledge, even new
holiness. For "it is given to us all alike, to catch the
glory of the Lord as in a mirror, with faces unveiled;
and so we become transfigured into the same likeness, borrowing glory from that glory, as the Spirit
of the Lord enables us" (II Cor. 3:18). This means,
of course, that a genuine Christian life is in itself a
continual *new song;* it is made so by a rich variety
of experience that is lived to the fullest depth and
vitalized by the varying graces imparted through the
mystery-events of the Church's liturgical cycle.

Thus vivified more and more with the life of the
risen Lord, all Christians not only should be moved
to heartfelt praise, but they also should become more
aware of an apostolic vocation to announce Christ's
salvation to those who sit in the shadow of unbelief
and ignorance. For an abiding sense of wonder ought
to impel all who have caught "the glory of the Lord"
to spread far and wide the "good news" of that amaz-

ing mystery which Christ has accomplished by His incarnation, death, and resurrection.

> Sing to the Lord a new song;
>   sing to the Lord, all you lands.
> Sing to the Lord; bless his name;
>   announce his salvation, day after day.
> Tell his glory among the nations;
>   among all peoples, his wondrous deeds.
> For great is the Lord and highly to be
>   praised;
>   and awesome is he, beyond all gods.
> For all the gods of the nations are things of
>   naught,
>   but the Lord made the heavens.
> Splendor and majesty go before him;
>   praise and grandeur are in his sanctuary.
>
> Give to the Lord, you families of nations,
>   give to the Lord glory and praise;
>   give to the Lord the glory due his name!

If this praise of the great mystery is really to nourish a person's inner life, it must be vitalized by that necessary attitude of soul, which consists in the continued emptying of self, so that God may fill the soul with His graces. Therefore, while Christ's members *worship* in the *holy attire* of heartfelt reverence, they must also express their attitude by the outward sign of *gifts* betokening self-surrender to His absolute dominion over their life and destiny.

> Bring gifts, and enter his courts;
>   worship the Lord in holy attire.
> Tremble before him, all the earth.

When through Christian prayer and sacrifice men will have come to acknowledge with conviction that *the Lord is king,* then they may hope to sing a truly *new song* in such a world as Pius XII envisioned when he wrote: "May the name of God as synonym for peace and freedom, be . . . the bond of peoples and nations, and the sign by which brothers and collaborators in the work of common salvation will recognize one another. . . . Above all, let His name re-echo in sacred temples and in hearts, . . . so that with His infinite power He may help to accomplish what weak human forces are having so much difficulty in attaining."

> Say among the nations: The Lord is king.
> He has made the world firm, not to be moved;
> he governs the peoples with equity.

Now, however, the Christian may call upon all nature, God's obedient servitor, to sing with him the *new song* of redemption being accomplished throughout the earth. For through him can the *heavens,* the *earth,* and the *sea,* even from their insentient being, raise the hymn of speechless joy and gratitude too often withheld by man with all his superlative natural endowments. Also the *trees of the forest,* by obeying their Maker's least behest may chant their soundless *song* of joy and fulfilment as they grow, unhindered by inward resistance, to the full stature of their God-given nature.

> Let the heavens be glad and the earth rejoice;

let the sea and what fills it resound;
let the plains be joyful and all that is in
them!
Then shall all the trees of the forest exult
before the Lord, for he comes.

Meanwhile, as the deified man prays and waits in
patience and faith for that grand fulfilment of the
redemptive work on earth, there is something else
he may and should be doing. The sun, the elements,
all living creatures, as well as the chain of events in
which they are involved—everything in the universe
has through the redemption taken on an eternal significance. That is to say, the essential meaning of
history is that the seed of eternity has already been
implanted in the womb of time and is awaiting its
delivery when the Lord of all creation returns with
power and glory to set up His Kingdom with a justice
no one will dare gainsay. And since in the psalms all
aspects of the redeeming act—past, present, and future—ever merge into one exultant cry of gladness
and gratitude, one may even now include in this *new
song* the wondrous mystery of Christ's last coming,
wherein may be discerned by faith the gates of
eternity already opened and God's everlasting Kingdom established. Here, then, is a fitting salute to the
eternal King:

For he comes to rule the earth.
He shall rule the world with justice
and the peoples with his constancy.

Psalm 96—God's Kingdom Has Come

I

The ninety-fifth Psalm closed on a note of the Lord's second coming; Psalm 96, with obvious continuity of thought, opens with the announcement that the Messianic throne is actually established, and the glorious reign has begun. That is, truth and righteousness triumphant, with all their divine potentiality, are already at work like a silent leaven in this world of time. For even now

The Lord is king; let the earth rejoice; let the many isles [souls] be glad.

For in all the myriad ways God may manifest Himself, He always imparts happiness to those who open their hearts to receive Him.

They must do this, however, amid the *darkness* of a faith whereby the mind accepts truths above and beyond any evidence of the senses. The more closely souls are united to God by grace, the more aware they are of the divine *clouds* of mystery enshrouding a God who transcends all human knowing. For in this mortal life man can discern but the imprint of His divine mind in the dispositions of His Providence which arranges all things in justice and equity.

Clouds and darkness are round about him, justice and judgment are the foundation of his throne.

But what of those who refuse to believe? Although divine love is an irresistible force that carries heavenward all souls who abandon themselves to its influence, it also wrecks any who would fain hug the ground of earthly attachments. For God's love becomes His wrath to those who withstand Him. Fire, symbol of His awful purity, blinds and consumes them instead of healing their darkness and purging away the impurities to which they cling.

> Fire goes before him
>   and consumes his foes round about.

While God's redeeming graces, scattered abroad with divine prodigality, *illumine* those who open their hearts, the *earth* of created love trembles when it sees all fleeting joys turned to ashes in its greedy hands. Then will the *mountains* of its hopes *melt like wax* because all things forsake them who have betrayed God's love.

> His lightnings illumine the world;
>   the earth sees and trembles.
> The mountains melt like wax before the
>   Lord,
>   before the Lord of all the earth.
> [For] the heavens proclaim his justice,
>   and all the peoples see his glory.

II

The second strophe of this poem is a logical deduction from the divine judgment just manifested. It shows that all who *worship* the idols of the modern world—luxuries, success, inordinate love—ought to recognize that in the light of Truth's eternity, these indeed are *things of naught*. Demanding as they do a whole life's devotedness, they repay it with only

the fruit of bitter disillusionment. Likewise, all creatures who have sought to set themselves up as *gods*,
basking in the adulation of the mindless mob—how
they will find themselves grovelling in the dust, when
the light of God's uncompromising truth reveals their
intrinsic nothingness.

> All who worship graven things are put to
>   shame,
>   who glory in the things of naught;
>   all gods are prostrate before him.

Then will all those who have long and patiently
awaited their beatitude rejoice exceedingly. For Sion
is built up of such as once hungered and thirsted for
justice, who gladly suffered persecution for the sake
of Him whom they believed, in blind and trusting
faith, to be *exalted* above all the gods of earth.

> Sion hears and is glad,
>   and the cities of Juda rejoice
>   because of your judgments, O Lord.
> Because you, O Lord, are the Most High
>   over all the earth,
>   exalted far above all gods.
> The Lord loves those that hate evil;
>   he guards the lives of his faithful ones;
>   from the hand of the wicked he delivers
>   them.

In this earthly life, although the final and definitive
judgment has not yet taken place, there is even now
much cause for joy. If one is *just*—i.e., not self-seeking
but eager for God's interests—there *dawns* a *light*
which reveals even to mortal minds the new creation
of redemptive love in all its splendor. This is that

kingdom set up by Christ and already come upon earth wherever hearts will receive it. Such souls become divinely luminous, like a radioactive substance, transforming into something new and splendid all with whom they come in contact. Christians, then, should rejoice even now because the new Kingdom of light and *gladness* has come upon earth like a consuming fire. And their privilege it is ever and everywhere to feed and extend this transforming flame of love and thankfulness.

> Light dawns for the just;
>   and gladness, for the upright of heart.
> Be glad in the Lord, you just,
>   and give thanks to his holy name.

Psalm 148—Needed Today: A Cosmic Song of Praise

In the "space age" with all its hitherto undreamed-of frontiers, there is greater need than ever before of acquiring a truly Christian mentality. This would integrate in a practical relationship with God all that is new and good in our amazing modern civilization. For, since man is no longer earth-bound in his plans and perspectives, there is great danger, amid all the scientific discoveries, that his universe may become like a room lit only from within by the feeble lamps of human knowledge, while the vast sunlight of supernatural truth is shut out. That need not happen, however, if only the modern mind can grasp something of the spirit of the ancient psalmist. His admiration of the natural wonders known in his day carried him out of himself in an ecstasy of praise, which is nothing else than the spontaneous expression of a heartfelt appreciation of things in relation to their Source. If that was true of one who marveled at the familiar phenomena of nature, how much greater should be the wonderment today at all the hitherto hidden prodigies whose discovery has been the special privilege of this present era. If the might of the surging sea aroused the psalmist to spontaneous praise of God's omnipotence reflected therein, how immeasurably greater should be man's admiration of such power and intelligence as could imprison all that stupendous energy in one infinitesimal atom.

Each new penetration into the long-hidden forces that surround this relatively small planet should likewise be a new insight into further depths of the infinite intelligence which could devise and construct the intricacies of laws that have taken the best of human minds a whole lifetime to discover. Yet that eternal Intellect could thus describe His own effortless solution to the problem of creative forces through His Word, the Wisdom that fashioned it all: "I was there when he built the heavens. . . . I was there when he . . . poised the foundations of the world. I was at his side, a master-workman, my delight increasing with each day, as I made play before him . . . in this world of dust" (Prov. 8:27-31).

The Lord has so constituted human nature that, when we admire something we instinctively break out into exclamations urging others to share the pleasure we have found: "Isn't that marvelous!" And this somehow adds to our own enjoyment. How inhibited we feel, on the other hand, if there is no one near to whom we can express our admiration of a beautiful picture, or our enthusiasm for a new book.

It would appear that our delight is not fully complete until it has found some outward form of expression; that praise, even on the natural level, not only fulfills our enjoyment but is its needed consummation. All this helps to explain why it is necessary for man to view with an appreciative eye the imprint in the world around him of the divine perfections: the infinite intelligence which devised the complexities of all the laws that govern nature's functioning; the splendor of the beauty reflected everywhere in symmetry and color; the surpassing harmony in the universe as it echoes the celestial harmonies emanating from the Triune God. Seen thus on the stereoscopic screen of faith and human knowledge, the whole cosmos may become one vast temple, where the Christian can act as high priest offering up all the silent, faithful worship of creation now vivified and ennobled through him, because he is praying Christ's own psalm of praise. For it has been said: "Upon our lips, as in the Word, . . . all these creatures become animate, [so] that they may sing the Creator's perfections."[1]

I

With such a hymn of praise the Christian can join himself at once to the heavenly choirs, those angelic spirits whose very existence is adoration. They give glory to the supreme Deity through their intuitive vision of God as the Cause of all things—a vision that penetrates and thrills them with adoring love.

---

[1] Columba Marmion, O.S.B., *Christ, the Ideal of the Monk* (St. Louis, Herder, 1926), p. 301.

> Praise the Lord from the heavens,
>   praise him in the heights;
> Praise him, all you his angels,
>   praise him, all you his hosts.

One can then turn to the song of praise sung unceasingly in the "music of the spheres" as they follow the immutable laws laid down for them, *the duty which shall not pass away*. Moreover, although modern man no longer views the highest *heavens* as the space above the firmament where the waters for precipitation are stored, he may nevertheless discover a profounder significance for the same term in the far more amazing forces that originate from a still more distant source and challenge his ingenuity to harness them for his own purposes. Yet these too should first be made to serve their Maker's glory by man's reverent knowledge, then by his use in accordance with the divine will.

> Praise him, sun and moon;
>   praise him, all you shining stars.
> Praise him, you highest heavens,
>   and you waters above the heavens.
> Let them praise the name of the Lord,
>   for he commanded and they were created;
> He established them forever and ever;
>   he gave them a duty which shall not pass
>   away.

II

Now all animal creation is given mind and voice, that, in the words of Bossuet, "it may love, in man and through him, the invisible beauty of the Creator. This is why he [man] is placed in the midst of the world," so that, contemplating all the lower creation and gathering it up in himself, "he may offer, sanctify, and consecrate it to the Living God."[1] Yet, regarding *sea monsters* and *depths,* only redeemed mankind would dare invoke them for praise according to their ancient symbolism, since they were figures of the vast evil that once held the world in thrall. But now in this era of redemption even they can be summoned to praise the Lord by acknowledging Christ's supremacy, as the Father "has put everything under his dominion" (Eph. 1:22).

So also, under the aegis of the Lord's kingship, His members may call upon all the elements of nature, seemingly lawless and untamed, which nevertheless always do God's will. Then one may recall that man, despite his materialistic outlook and shameless exploitation, still has not lost his headship over the lower orders of creation. Therefore now, with a corresponding resolve henceforth to use God's gifts more in accordance with His designs, the Christian may learn to lift up in their Maker's praise not only the grandeur of the *mountains,* or the *fruit trees'* prodigality. He may even stop to wonder at the tender carefulness of that infinite Intelligence that could stoop to fashion the lowly *creeping things;* and with consummate art did He blend the gorgeous plumage of the birds.

> Praise the Lord from the earth,
>   you sea monsters and all depths;

---

[1] Sermon for the Feast of the Annunciation, 1662.

Fire and hail, snow and mist,
    storm winds that fulfill his word;
You mountains and all you hills,
    you fruit trees and all you cedars;
You wild beasts and all tame animals,
    you creeping things and you winged fowl.

III

That the psalms are indeed the voice of the Mystic Christ is made abundantly clear in the last strophe, which constitutes a roll call of all His members on earth, summoning them to add their voices to the universal hymn of praise. Thus acting, man not only enters into the very life of the Holy Trinity, where the Word is ever an "eternal sacrifice" of praise; but he may also taste of everlasting bliss in this worship, which should even now be a thing of joy. There are other considerations, too, that ought to make all redeemed mankind fall upon its knees and there live a life of enduring adoration. For in this era of His risen victory, Christ has restored to *his people* superhuman strength and courage under the figure of the animal *horn*; this was always to ancient minds a symbol of power.

Above all, in this "new creation" established by His saving death, Christ has lifted up a fallen race to share in His own divine life. The psalm enumerates such beneficiaries who should in justice as well as love pay Him the homage of their whole being: 1) those who by His grace are ever *faithful* to His gifts despite the roughness of the way they must tread; 2) the new *children of Israel,* who in their adopted sonship "follow the leading of God's Spirit [and] are all God's sons" (Rom. 8:14). Lastly those owe Him most praise who have become a *people close to him* by having eaten of His vivifying Flesh and who therefore so abide in Him that they can exclaim with St. Paul: "True, I am living, here and now, this mortal life; but my real life is the faith I have in the Son of God, who loved me, and gave himself for me" (Gal. 2:20).

> Let the kings of the earth and all peoples,
> > the princes and all the judges of the earth,
> Young men too, and maidens,
> > old men and boys,
> Praise the name of the Lord,
> > for his name alone is exalted;
> His majesty is above earth and heaven,
> > and he has lifted up the horn of his people.
> Be this his praise from all his faithful ones,
> > from the children of Israel, the people close to him.

Psalm 149—Self-Conquest, the Holocaust of Praise

Nothing in the whole history of the Jewish people so deeply impressed them as their having been twice liberated by divine intervention from slavery to a foreign power. After the escape from Pharaoh through their miraculous passage of the Red Sea, they were so delirious with joy that they sang and danced their praises of the Lord. But centuries later, when Israel came home from the Babylonian exile, their celebration contained an element of restraint, since the "remnant" had learned through suffering to look into the depths of the mystery and to find that ultimate victory over evil is won, not by God alone but through man's faithful cooperation with God. Likewise Christians today, while realizing the Savior's decisive victory in freeing them from their slavery to the Prince of this World, also perceive in this mystery of redemption a conquest that each must also help to achieve in the sector of his own soul. Like the Israelites returned from their Babylonian exile, all who have been reborn in Christ must build up the walls of Christendom while warding off hidden attacks of an enemy who jealously resents every success.

I

The grim backdrop of Israel's return from Babylon, which most commentators think was the origin of this psalm, does not lessen, however, the supreme joy which every Christian should feel at the thought of the redemption, of which the restoration was a figure. In fact, every day ought to be a *new song* of thankfulness and praise, because the graces flowing from the cross are as new and varied as life itself. Moreover, this psalm is a summons to praise *in the assembly of the faithful.* That is, among all those who, having renounced Satan, have come home, at least in will and intent, from mankind's long exile of this-worldliness to help rebuild the temple of God's rightful worship by trying to "live and move in a new kind of existence" (Rom. 6:4). What else could this mean but, first of all, to contemplate the eternal

verities: that the Lord is King and rules in peace and
love.

> Sing to the Lord a new song
>   of praise in the assembly of the faithful.
> Let Israel be glad in their maker,
>   let the children of Sion rejoice in their
>   king.

Just what form should this Christian rejoicing
today assume? What are its underlying dispositions?
First and foremost, complete abandonment to the
divine will directing all of man's multiform activities.
Though to view these thus may be disconcerting at
first, they really constitute one great cosmic *dance*,
with God Himself as the inimitable Choreographer.
For who but infinite Wisdom ever could work out the
multitudinous patterns of men's self-willed lives into
such a world-compassing design that spells God's
ultimate glory?

Then the psalmist also intimates that souls who
praise the Lord should be like *timbrel* and *harp*,
passive instruments on which the divine Musician
may play. How useless these would be, however,
if the drum were so filled with self as to lose its
resonance for spiritual things, or if the harp of the
soul, with strings of heaven-lent capacities, were
jangled and out of tune by reason of its own self-
seeking. Such souls should ever bear in mind that the
hand of the Lord strikes only in love, so that He may
exalt them actually to participate in His own song
of victory.

> Let them praise his name in the festive
>   dance,

let them sing praise to him with timbrel
   and harp.
For the Lord loves his people,
   and he adorns the lowly with victory.

Unfortunately, the truth that Christ alone could
and did accomplish man's redemption has sometimes
given rise to the false notion that His payment of
sufferings was complete for all time and all men.
True, He did wipe out the guilt of the whole world
and create an abundance of grace that is always
available. Nevertheless, every man born in Christ to
the new life as God's son, must have his passion to
undergo for both his own and the world's salvation.
Consequently, even while exulting in the *glory* of
the Savior's redeeming work, Christians may now
sing for joy upon their couches for only the briefest
respite. That is, they may not be smug over any personal achievements with a sense of final accomplishment, since only the over-all power of the enemy has
been broken. He does not cease to wage guerilla warfare through temptations lurking in every concu-
piscence-ridden soul.

   Let the faithful exult in glory;
      let them sing for joy upon their couches;
      let the high praises of God be in their
         throats.

II

The Prince of Peace, who when taken prisoner
would not raise up a single angel in His own self-
defense, once said to the people, "I have come to

bring a sword, not peace" (Matt. 10:34). This means
that anyone calling himself Christian must be armed
with a two-edged sword to wield on himself until
it reaches "the very division between soul and spirit,
between joints and marrow, quick to distinguish
every thought and design in our hearts" (Heb. 4:12).
For the ultimate victory of each redeemed soul depends upon the energy with which it seeks out and
kills every foe lurking within its own domain. Thus
one must *execute vengeance* on the heathen, unre-
generate tendencies in human nature that have already inflicted many defeats. For who is there living
today that cannot testify with St. Paul: "It is not
the good my will prefers, but the evil my will dis-
approves, that I find myself doing" (Rom. 7:19)?
Also those passions that have usurped the ruling
power must be *bound with* the *iron fetters* of stern
self-denial. Though all these hostile forces are under
written sentence of death by reason of Christ's decisive victory, it is indeed the *glory* of the *faithful*
to play their part in executing that sentence, each
one within the kingdom of his own soul.

Such individual conquest, however, is but an infinitesimal share in Christ's own triumph. Yet it
does entitle the creature-victor to reach the borders
of the Promised Land—eternity—and there to hear
the royal Conqueror's own welcoming commenda-
tion: "Well done, my good and faithful servant; . . .
come and share the joy of thy Lord" (Matt. 25:23).

> And let two-edged swords be in their hands:
>   to execute vengeance on the nations,
>   punishments on the peoples;

To bind their kings with chains,
   their nobles with fetters of iron;
To execute on them the written sentence.
This is the glory of all his faithful.
                                    Alleluia.

Psalm 150—All Humanity's Symphony of Praise

The Psalter began with an invitation to meditate
on the *law* of the Lord, which means nothing less
than "communion with [Him] through the adoption
of His own thoughts."[1] These have been revealed
with an infinite condescension and intimacy in all
His inspired songs, from the nature poems reflecting His magnificence and beauty, to the battle hymns
revealing His immanence in human history as He
champions His own in their great struggle with the
powers of evil. Even more, through His Word the
Lord has revealed to men how they may seek Him in
difficulties so as to turn each petty trouble into a thing
of grandeur that can help toward making themselves
and others a "new people." All such experience of
the mystery of God's creating and redeeming love
has meant that, taking the Old-Testament expression
as the starting point, Christians should expand their
spiritual penetration into an ever deeper and wider
realization, until they are illumined through and
through, not only by the Promise but with an intense
desire for its ultimate fulfilment.

This is possible for even the "ordinary Christian"
because the Word of God is also a creative force. It
not only reveals the All-Holy but has the intrinsic

---

[1] Louis Bouyer, *The Meaning of Sacred Scripture* (South Bend, Ind.,
University of Notre Dame Press, 1958), p. 22.

power to bring about the fulfilment of His will made known even today through Sacred Scripture, of which the Psalter is a beautiful compendium. Therefore, as one learns more and more to live his life on a deeper level in union with the hidden presence there, he will discover that such a life-with-God is summed up in one word—surrender. To be ever at God's disposal in all things is but the creature's "reasonable service" and its response of love to the divine espousal celebrated in Psalm 44.

It should not be surprising, then, to find that the last of the psalms is an ultimate expression of the spirituality gained by a Christian who has assiduously meditated them. Even though painfully aware of his many ingrained faults and habitual failings, such a one should rightfully feel himself drawn to the complete gift of self; for this is the only fitting praise for the God whose *sovereign majesty* is infinitely far removed from man's sinful creaturehood. That is what St. Thérèse had in mind when she wrote of her life at Carmel as a song telling over and over again the Lord's wondrous mercies (Ps. 88:1). So too should all Christians, saints and sinners, make their lives a symphony of praise by each one's offering himself as an instrument on which Christ may play that most perfect hymn of worship, His own song of the redemption.

This means that He must be free to choose some souls to do great deeds for Him; to be, as it were, *trumpets* whose blast resounds world-wide down the centuries. Yet to other souls He may assign the part of sounding only sweet melodies of kindly deeds, like those of the *lyre* or *harp*, which are heard merely by a few. Still others the divine Musician may use

as *timbrels,* whose life-hymn is but the dull, monot-
onous thud of menial tasks amid drab surroundings
that only a supernatural faith could enhance with joy
and beauty. Others again may be given the role of
crashing cymbals, as they bravely clang their dis-
cordant opposition to the shallowness that drains
their time and energies, the giving to Caesar so much
that is rightfully God's. Then too the Lord sometimes
permits His orchestra to play with *strings* and *pipe*
just a scherzo for *dance* and light-hearted merriment.
For it is not what His instruments do, but the love
and selflessness that go into the doing which makes
the music of this tenfold *Alleluia.*

Alleluia, "praise God," really means to radiate
the Lord—i.e., to become radioactive with supernatural light and life by reason of being vitalized
through intimate contact with the Word as He has
given Himself to men in the Psalter. Having thus
nourished heart and mind through personal prayer,
the Christian should have come to know "in all its
breadth and length and height and depth" (Eph.
3:19) the mystery of God's creating and redeeming
love. Then the soul may realize that its answer to the
Word freely imparted can be fully given only when
the Word itself is rendered back to God in the psalms
of praise.

Now indeed a wondrous transposition takes place
by the divine power, a gradual transition not only
from Old-Testament figure to New-Testament fulfilment, but also from the transitory images of earth
to the eternal reality of the vision described by St.
John under the figure of a vast liturgy. That the choirs
of earth are even now truly united with those of

heaven is clear from this scene: in the very center
of all the celestial glory stands Christ, our Head,
wearing His wounds yet triumphant. And since in
Him the glory came down and lifted man up to share
His very life, man's earthly homage of praise also
is present with Christ now throned in transcendent
splendor. And so it is that earth's symphony of adoration even now resounds amid those heavenly choirs
whose golden bowls are "full of incense, the prayers
of the saints" (Apoc. 5:8).

> Praise the Lord in his sanctuary,
>   praise him in the firmament of his strength.
> Praise him for his mighty deeds,
>   praise him for his sovereign majesty.
> Praise him with the blast of the trumpet,
>   praise him with lyre and harp,
> Praise him with timbrel and dance,
>   praise him with strings and pipe.
> Praise him with sounding cymbals,
>   praise him with clanging cymbals.
> Let everything that has breath
>   praise the Lord. Alleluia.